HUGH WINEBRENNER

★★★★★★★★★★★★★★★

The Iowa Precinct Caucuses

The Making of a Media Event

★★★★★★★★★★★★★★★★★★★★★★★★★★★★★★★★★

HUGH WINEBRENNER

 Iowa State University Press / Ames

For my parents

★★★★★ Mabel and Bert Winebrenner

Hugh Winebrenner is Professor of Public Administration,
Drake University, Des Moines, Iowa.

© 1987 Iowa State University Press, Ames, Iowa 50010
All rights reserved

Composed by Iowa State University Press from author-provided disks
Printed in the United States of America

First edition, 1987

Library of Congress Cataloging-in-Publication Data

Winebrenner, Hugh, 1937–
    The Iowa precinct caucuses.

    Includes index.
    1. Presidents—United States—Nomination. 2. Mass media—Political aspects—
United States. 3. Press and politics—United States. 4. Political parties—Iowa. 5.
Iowa—Politics and government. I. Title.
JK521.W55   1987   324.5′2   87-3383
ISBN 0–8138–1001–9

Contents

Preface

People in other parts of the country are occasionally confused as to Iowa's location on the map, but political reporters in the national press corps have no difficulty pinpointing the state. Though some waggish visitors still refer to Iowa as the state that is "overplowed and overcowed," political observers now refer to Iowa as a kingmaker in presidential politics.

In fact, a political accident in the early 1970s propelled Iowa onto the front pages of the nation's newspapers and prime-time coverage on national news shows. Because the Iowa Democrats needed some breathing space in their caucus and convention schedule, they pushed forward the precinct caucuses in 1972. As it turned out, the caucuses became the first presidential nominating event in the nation. Politicos both within and outside of Iowa quickly realized the impact of this new status, and along with the national media, they promoted Iowa's caucuses with a vengeance.

This book is about the Iowa precinct caucuses—how they began, how they changed, and how they have been manipulated to become a national media event. The caucuses have gained their significant position in the presidential electoral process despite the fact that they do not produce meaningful results. The nationally reported "results" are contrived by the Iowa parties to portray a desired picture of the process, and on one occasion they were of such questionable validity that even party officials were unable to guarantee their accuracy.

The Iowa precinct caucuses are essentially local party functions that have been manipulated into the position of making or breaking presidential candidacies by the media, the political parties, and the presidential candidates themselves. Essentially, the caucuses have become a media event with an impact on presidential politics totally out of proportion to the reality of their purpose or procedural methods. Thomas E. Patterson and Michael J. Robinson in the 1970s and 1980s have been at the forefront of researchers examining the impact of the media on the national electoral process—at the same time that Iowa was gaining national prominence due to its first-in-the-nation status in presidential politics. Drawing heavily on the groundbreaking theories of these authors, this work uses Iowa as the premier case study to examine the role of the media in the American electoral process.

The book is divided into eight chapters. Chapters 1 through 3 provide historical and demographic information about Iowa, including an analysis of Iowa's political culture. Chapter 4 contrasts the local character of the 1968 caucuses with the 1972 caucuses, which focused a national spotlight on George McGovern as he began his quest for the Democratic presidential nomination. The changes in the procedures followed in both parties' caucuses that were required to accommodate media needs for outcomes are detailed. Chapter 5 analyzes how phony "results" from the Democratic precinct caucuses in 1976 changed the political fortunes of Jimmy Carter from unknown to frontrunner. Chapter 6 analyzes the 1980 precinct caucuses as a media event of grandiose proportions. Republican precinct data reveal that George Bush's emergence as a challenger to Ronald Reagan was based on media perceptions drawn from a preference poll that he may or may not have won. Chapter 7 analyzes the 1984 precinct caucuses and the numerous associated controversies. Chapter 8 attempts to place the caucuses in some perspective.

In this book, then, I argue that the reporting of the Iowa caucus results is part of the game focus of presidential campaigns. Essentially meaningless caucus outcomes are reported to satisfy the media's needs for "hard data" about the progress of the presidential race.

Acknowledgments

I received a great deal of assistance in the conduct of this project. I am indebted to Richard Schultze of the state law library for research on the *Code of Iowa*. A number of graduate assistants from Drake University's Master of Public Administration program contributed to this research. The most significant contributor, Kelly Brodie, may have perused more editions of local and national newspapers than most full-time newspaper archivists. Debra Moore, Debra Sears, Martha Gelhaus, Tracie Washington, Jeffrey Martins, and David Unmacht also made significant contributions. The officials and staff of both state parties were very forthcoming and extremely helpful throughout the project. Colleagues Frank Wilhoit and Mark Peffley commented on parts of the book. Most important, my wife, Nancy, read and commented on every page of the manuscript at least twice, and her questions and comments added immeasurably to its focus and readability. Any errors that remain are, of course, my own.

List of Tables

The Iowa Precinct Caucuses
The Making of a Media Event

★★★★★ **1** ★★★★★★★★★

The Media and American Politics: An Introduction

Prior to the 1970s, studies of elections and voting behavior by political scientists paid relatively little attention to the role of the media in elections in the United States. The seminal study of electoral behavior, *The American Voter* (1960), devoted few pages to the mass media or their impact on election outcomes. Most of the early studies concluded that the media's effects were not of primary importance and focused on party loyalty and attitudes about the issues to explain electoral choice (Patterson 1980, vii).

The growth of television news coverage in the 1960s and increased media interest in the nomination of the president, particularly in direct primary elections, stimulated research on the role of the media in electoral politics. Although Florida established the direct primary for the selection of national convention delegates in 1904, followed closely by Wisconsin in 1905 (Ranney 1977, 4), the presidential nominating process was dominated by party leaders until very recently. The existence of a relatively short primary campaign in less than half of the states did not promote the democratic nature of the process to the

Portions of this work were previously published as "The Iowa Precinct Caucuses: The Making of a Media Event," in the *Southeastern Political Review* 13 (1985): 99–132. Used by permission.

extent that early-twentieth-century progressives had hoped. Rather, party leaders, although periodically inconvenienced by primary elections, continued to dominate the nomination of presidential candidates through the caucus and convention system utilized in most states (Crotty and Jackson 1985, 13–18).

In the 1960s the direct primary assumed a more prominent role in the selection of the president and began to pose a challenge to the control exercised by party leaders through the caucus and convention system. Several factors contributed to the democratization of the nominating process. Presidential candidates, particularly those who lacked the support of party chieftains in important states, increasingly attempted to demonstrate their voter appeal in primary elections. Although early attempts by Harold Stassen in 1948 and Estes Kefauver in 1952 to gain their parties' nomination via primary elections proved unsuccessful, the increased emphasis on the primaries by presidential candidates contributed to their becoming the dominant component of the nominating process. It was not long before presidential candidates had first to demonstrate their voter appeal in primary elections (Davis 1967, 3–5).

The growth of media coverage, particularly television, was largely responsible for turning presidential primaries into a uniquely American political olympic contest. Although common now, comprehensive television coverage of the presidential primaries dates only to the 1960s. Television provides a viable, cost-effective alternative to the face-to-face contact between candidates and voters previously considered so important in American political campaigns. Moreover, by providing presidential hopefuls with a means of bypassing the party leadership and appealing directly to ordinary citizens, television focused the nominating process on the candidates themselves rather than on the activities of political party leaders (Davis 1967, 5–9). Austin Ranney concludes that "the advent of television as the principal source of political reality for most

Americans has altered the political game profoundly, perhaps more profoundly than all the parties' rules changes and new state and federal laws put together." Furthermore, "it has had an enormous impact on the kinds of persons who become successful politicians and on how they conduct their business" (Ranney 1983, 89).

An additional democratizing factor in the presidential nominating process was the series of party rules changes undertaken by the national Democratic party beginning in 1968 and continuing into the 1980s (Crotty and Jackson 1985, chap. 2). The new rules were designed to increase the impact of citizen participation and to limit the role of party leaders at all levels of the delegate selection process.

The new party rules succeeded in further diminishing the role of party leaders and centering attention on the primary elections. During the period from 1968 to 1980 the presidential primary was very much in vogue, and the number of states selecting national convention delegates by primary elections grew dramatically. (Democratic party primaries increased in number from seventeen to thirty-five and selected 72 percent of the 1980 convention delegates. Republican primaries grew in number from sixteen to thirty-four and selected 76 percent of the 1980 convention delegates [Crotty and Jackson 1985, 63].)

But not everyone viewed the primary movement as a positive development. By 1980 party leaders and elected officials were being excluded in increasing numbers from the national conventions, which now did little more than ratify the results of the primary elections. Dissatisfaction increased to the point that by 1984 the primary election trend had been reversed; only twenty-five states held binding Democratic primaries, compared to thirty-five in 1980, and only thirty conducted Republican presidential primaries, a loss of four states (Crotty and Jackson 1985, 63). According to the *National Journal*, party officials had become increasingly "concerned that the proliferation of primaries was largely responsible for the prolonged, costly, divisive, and media-dominated campaigns and that they further served to undermine organized party control" (1983, 2215). The renewed interest in the caucus and convention system, however, may represent a final effort on the part of state party organizations to save themselves from extinction.

Media-dominated, candidate-centered presidential campaigns have stimulated research into the role of the media in political campaigns. Most studies have concentrated on presidential campaigns, and their areas of research include the media's emphasis on a candidate's "image" (Nimmo and Savage 1976), the media as kingmakers (Paletz and Entman 1981; Graber 1980; Patterson 1980; Ranney 1983), and media influence on the campaign strategies of candidates (Arterton 1984; Barber 1978; Robinson and Sheehan 1983).

Recent studies indicate that the media have replaced political parties as the "main link between presidential candidates and the overwhelming majority of the public" (Paletz and Entman 1981, 32). As a consequence, political parties have become less significant in electoral politics. The modern presidential race is a media campaign, "and campaign managers believe, almost uniformly, that their most efficient means of persuasive communication is these pre-established communications media" (Arterton 1984, 1).

Citizens may be passive consumers of electoral politics and may pay little attention to political parties, but with their televisions playing six to seven hours a day, it is very difficult for average citizens to ignore presidential campaigns. The broadcast media in particular give Americans the opportunity to assess the presidential hopefuls personally, even though they may simply be evaluating their Madison Avenue images. Furthermore, the media seem to have altered the two-step flow of political information, in which information and opinions are transmitted first from elites to attentive publics and from them to citizen voters (Katz and Lazarsfeld 1955). Today the media seem to have assumed the role formerly played by political parties, and the political "reality" consists of the information transmitted from elites to the public by way of the news media.

Research also indicates that the news media play a major role in agenda setting in American electoral politics by determining which candidates the public should take seriously (Robinson and Sheehan 1983, 262–72). Presidential candidates that media correspondents perceive to be viable, serious contenders are portrayed as such and receive extensive coverage. Those whose candidacies are judged to be frivolous or unlikely to succeed find it difficult to gain coverage. The task for presidential hopefuls becomes one of persuading reporters that their candidacies should be taken seriously and covered regularly. In the 1970s and 1980s they have often accomplished this by exceeding the media's expectations in polls, primary elections, and caucuses.

The news media, and television in particular, influence the form as well as the content of electoral politics. As a visual medium, television tends to emphasize candidates or, more specifically, images of candidates that they either create or help to develop (Robinson and Sheehan 1983, 269–70). Both President Gerald Ford's clumsiness, though he had a strong athletic background, and John F. Kennedy's vigor, though he suffered from back problems that limited his physical activity, are images created and nurtured by the media. In the modern presidential race, style is substance, and since most potential voters cannot experience political campaigns directly, they rely on the media to delimit and interpret the substance of campaigns.

The news media have become increasingly important in American electoral politics in the last twenty years. They have enormous impact on both the content and the form of political campaigns, influencing who chooses to run for the presidency and how they conduct their campaigns. Style and image have become the substance of politics as the broadcast and print media have replaced political parties as the principal linkage between presidential hopefuls and the voters.

This book will examine the media's impact on the Iowa precinct caucuses and the significant role the caucuses have assumed in the presidential nominating process. By highlighting the Iowa caucuses as the first nominating event in the presidential race, the news media have centered national attention on the caucuses and have profoundly affected the process itself. With the enthusiastic cooperation of the officials of the Iowa Democratic and Republican parties, the media have influenced when and how the Iowa caucuses have conducted their business and, in the process, have created a media event. In an article on the media's impact on the presidential nominating process, Michael Robinson coined the term *mediality* to describe "events, developments, or situations to which the media have given importance by emphasizing, expanding, or featuring them in such a way that their real significance has been modified, distorted, or obscured" (Robinson 1981, 191).

The Iowa precinct caucuses provide a dramatic example of media events, or medialities in Robinson's terminology. The media have obscured the basic local functions of the caucuses—selecting delegates to county conventions, generating issues for party platforms, and providing the grass-roots party connections to the citizens—by attributing a meaning to caucuses that does not exist. The media's tendency to interpret Iowa caucus "results" as "hard news" about the progress of the presidential campaign is at best questionable. At worst, media exploitation of the Iowa caucus process (1) disrupts the normal functioning of the local political process, (2) may give a false image of the national political appeal of the candidates involved, and (3) subjects the national electoral process to the influence of a contrived event.

Thomas Patterson provides an interesting explanation of the media's motivation in emphasizing events like the Iowa caucuses. His systematic analysis of the 1976 presidential election suggests that media distortion of the Iowa caucuses stems from a structural bias in the way presidential elections are covered. Patterson's content analysis of

The larger states are unhappy that Iowa and New Hampshire have emerged as kingmakers in the presidential nominating process. Although many states have moved their primary events closer to the beginning of the nominating season, Iowa and New Hampshire continue to deliver knockout blows in the bout for the presidency.

news reports of the presidential nominating process provides clear evidence of the media's tendency to exaggerate the "game" aspects of the campaign (Patterson 1980, 22–24). Since media interest centers around who is winning and who is losing the game, the candidates' strategies and tactics are emphasized at the expense of the substance of the campaigns: the public problems, the policy debates, and the candidates' leadership qualities. Patterson forcefully argues that the bias in selecting "newsworthy" events has more to do with the interests of the media—conflict, drama, measurable outcomes—than the reality of the campaign. He demonstrates that media bias influences the public's image of presidential campaigns and perhaps their voting behavior.

The reporting of Iowa caucus results is a part of the game focus of presidential campaigns: essentially meaningless caucus outcomes are reported to satisfy the media's need for results or hard news. Further, the media not only report the outcome of the primary games, they also interpret the outcomes for the American public in terms of the expectations that the media themselves often had helped to create (Patterson 1980, 43–48). Much like the handicapper in a horse race, the media assign metaphorical labels—such as favorite, front-runner, long shot, or dark horse—to the presidential candidates and then evaluate their performance in caucuses and primary elections according to the expectations created by the labels. Meeting or exceeding media expectations is crucial to the campaigns of presidential candidates. Since 1972 Iowa has been the first major event in the presidential nominating game, and media expectations and interpretations of caucus outcomes have made Iowa a very important component of the game.

This case study will focus on changes in the Iowa precinct caucuses since 1972 which have been associated with their becoming a media event and will examine the caucuses as part of the presidential nominating game. It will explore the profound impact of the mass media both on the Iowa precinct caucuses and on the presidential nominating system generally. As such, this study is a special case of the broader public problem of setting the public agenda through media initiatives, in this instance the agenda for the presidential nominating process. It is argued that since the media choose to emphasize the outcomes of early nominating events, Iowa plays a major role in setting the presidential nominating agenda, perhaps to the disadvantage of the country.

References

Arterton, F. Christopher. 1984. *Media Politics: The News Strategies of Presidential Campaigns*. Lexington, Mass.: Lexington Books.

Barber, James D., ed. 1978. *Race for the Presidency: The Media and the Nominating Process*. Englewood Cliffs, N.J.: Prentice-Hall.

Campbell, Angus, Philip E. Converse, Warren E. Miller, and Donald E. Stokes. 1960. *The American Voter*. New York: John Wiley and Sons.

Crotty, William. 1984. *American Parties in Decline*. 2d ed. Boston: Little, Brown.

Crotty, William, and John S. Jackson III. 1985. *Presidential Primaries and Nominations*. Washington, D.C.: CQ Press.

Davis, James W. 1967. *Presidential Primaries: Road to the White House*. New York: Thomas Y. Crowell.

Graber, Doris A. 1980. *Mass Media and American Politics*. Washington, D.C.: CQ Press.

Katz, Elihu, and Paul F. Lazarsfeld. 1955. *Personal Influence: The Part Played by People in the Flow of Mass Communications*. New York: Free Press.

National Journal. 1983. *Election '84 Handbook: A Guide to the Candidates, the Issues, and the Voters*. Washington, D.C.: Government Research Corp.

Nimmo, Dan, and Robert L. Savage. 1976. *Candidates and Their Images: Concepts, Methods, and Findings*. Pacific Palisades, Calif.: Goodyear.

Paletz, David L., and Robert M. Entman. 1981. *Media, Power, Politics.* New York: Free Press.

Patterson, Thomas E. 1980. *The Mass Media Election: How Americans Choose Their President.* New York: Praeger.

Ranney, Austin. 1977. *Participation in American Presidential Nominations, 1976.* Washington, D.C.: American Enterprise Institute.

_____. 1983. *Channels of Power: The Impact of Television on American Politics.* New York: Basic Books.

Robinson, Michael J. 1981. "The Media in 1980: Was the Message the Message?" In *The American Elections of 1980,* edited by Austin Ranney, 177–211. Washington, D.C.: American Enterprise Institute.

Robinson, Michael J., and Margaret A. Sheehan. 1983. *Over the Wire and on TV: CBS and UPI in Campaign '80.* New York: Russell Sage Foundation.

Wattenberg, Martin P. 1984. *The Decline of American Political Parties, 1952–1980.* Cambridge, Mass.: Harvard Univ. Press.

2

Iowa: A Political and Demographic Profile

Is Iowa a good place to start the presidential campaign? Is it a representative state? Is it more representative than New Hampshire, the traditional early king-maker of presidential politics? Party officials in Iowa—and some national writers—have asserted that Iowa is a good place to kick off the presidential campaign because it is a two-party state known for its clean politics. Moreover, its hardworking people take their duties as citizens very seriously. Finally, the state is small enough that less well known and less well financed presidential hopefuls have a chance, through hard work and good organization, to establish themselves as viable candidates. These assertions have for the most part developed after the fact; that is, as an attempt to rationalize the role Iowa has assumed in presidential politics. Furthermore, these arguments ignore the fact that Iowa gained its first-in-the-nation status accidentally.

This chapter examines the political and demographic characteristics of Iowa and shows that although it is clean and competitive, Iowa is not a microcosm of the nation. The lack of representativeness works to the advantage of some candidates and to the disadvantage of others, and in the process it may mislead the nation about the progress of a presidential campaign.

There is no current literature on the political culture of

13

HAVE YOUR PICTURE
TAKEN WITH A
Genuine Iowa Pig.
15% DISCOUNT FOR
PRESIDENTIAL
CANDIDATES!

There are certain rituals that all presidential candidates follow in their early campaign visits to Iowa. They spend time with officials of the state parties in Des Moines, and they visit the state capitol where they often speak to a party caucus of the house of representatives or the senate. Perhaps most popular of the Iowa rituals is a visit to a farm where the candidate is photographed—in his new coveralls, boots, and a cap from one of the seed companies—intently gazing into a hog pen.

Iowa. In 1968 Samuel C. Patterson, a leading scholar, characterized the dominant political style of Iowa as "highly pragmatic, non-programmatic, cautious and moderate" (202), a description that continues to be accurate. Unlike its northern neighbors, Wisconsin and Minnesota, Iowa has seldom been in the vanguard of progressive change, but neither has it lagged far behind other states. Within the state, particularly in rural areas, politics can be very conservative (as in Butler and Grundy counties, for example), but they are balanced by the moderate, and occasionally liberal, politics of urban areas, which include a majority of the state's population.

As Iowa's urban population surpassed that of its rural areas, the urban-rural cleavage documented in the early 1970s has grown (Hahn 1971). The general assembly was dominated by rural representatives until the 1970 reapportionment required by the "one man, one vote" decisions of the U.S. Supreme Court.[1] Since reapportionment, urban representation in the general assembly has increased dramatically, and the urban-rural conflict is more pronounced. The cleavage is evident in the representatives' behavior and their attitudes toward government and public activity in general. It can also be seen in the laws passed by the legislature, which frequently include urban-rural formulas for the allocation of state funds. Examples range from the use of road trust funds to recent legislation allocating receipts of the newly created state lottery.

But how did Iowa politics come to be "highly pragmatic, non-programmatic, cautious and moderate"? Political institutions do not spring full-blown from the minds of philosophers, nor are patterns of political behavior explainable solely on the basis of their internal characteristics. Rather, they are products of the total environment of a so-

1. Baker v. Carr, 369 U.S. 258 (1962); Wesberry v. Sanders, 376 U.S. 1 (1964); Reynolds v. Sims, 377 U.S. 533 (1964). For a discussion of the reapportionment of Iowa congressional and legislative districts, see "Legislative Reapportionment" *Iowa Official Register 1965–66*, 1965, 113–18; also see the 1968 and 1970 amendments to the Iowa Constitution.

ciety and can be fully understood only in terms of other patterns of rational behavior. In his book on American federalism, Daniel Elazar identifies three factors that are important in shaping the political structures, functions, and behavior of American states: sectionalism, the continuing frontier, and the political culture.

Sectionalism refers to "the more or less permanent political ties that link together groups of contiguous states with bonds of shared interests" (Elazar 1984, 109). Sectionalism helps us to understand the geographic differences in state responses to national political, social, and economic initiatives and activities. Sectionally, Iowa is identified with the agricultural heartland of the north central portion of the country. It is probable, however, that the sectional basis of American politics was significantly reduced by the partisan realignment President Franklin D. Roosevelt caused in the 1930s (Jewell and Olson 1982, 22–23).

The idea of a continuing frontier concerns the ongoing effort of Americans to control their environment, which results in a periodic reorganization of social and settlement patterns. Elazar identifies four stages that the American frontier has passed through. The "rural-land" or "westward ho" movement associated with the classic American frontier from the seventeenth through the nineteenth centuries gave rise to the family farm and a socioeconomic system based on agriculture. The second stage, the "urban-industrial" frontier of the nineteenth century, transformed America into an industrial nation in which the cities, which had always depended on agriculture, became independent industrial centers. Third, the mid–twentieth century "metropolitan-technological" frontier was brought on by rapidly changing technologies and is characterized by the suburbanization of America. Finally, the "rurban-cybernetic" frontier emerged in the 1980s and is "based on cybernetic technologies developed on the metropolitan frontier" (Elazar 1984, 123–26).

Although the latter frontiers have had an impact on

Iowa, the social, economic, and political attitudes of the state are still deeply rooted in the "rural-land" period of an earlier day. Limited migration into the state and modest growth have contributed to a stable, although more urbanized, population. A commitment to the land, particularly to the family farm, and to small towns and local financial institutions and a distrust and fear of "big cities" (Des Moines, Cedar Rapids, and Davenport, with populations of over 100,000, are viewed as big cities) are deeply ingrained in the psyche of many Iowans (*Iowa Poll: 1986*, poll no. 1254).[2]

Elazar's third factor, political culture, is very important in any attempt to understand politics, and it provides a focus for further discussion. Political culture is that set of learned values, beliefs, and expectations that orient people to the political systems of which they are members. It has its roots in the cumulative historical experience of particular groups. Since values, beliefs, and expectations are learned, political culture is consciously or unconsciously passed on from generation to generation. The political culture influences political practice in a number of ways. It shapes citizens' perceptions and expectations of politics, it defines which activities may legitimately be undertaken by government, it helps determine the kinds of people who are active in government and politics, and it shapes the practices of government. It is, in other words, the conscience and ethics of a political system and its actors (Elazar 1984, 112).

American political culture, according to Elazar, "is a synthesis of three major political subcultures that jointly inhabit the country, existing side by side or even overlapping." These are the individualistic, moralistic, and traditionalistic subcultures, and they are tied to specific sections of the country (Elazar 1984, 114). The moralistic

2. The Iowa Poll, conducted by the *Des Moines Register*, claims to be the nation's oldest statewide poll. It conforms to the standards of the National Council on Public Polls. All polls used in this work have margins of error in the range of plus or minus 3 to 5 percent.

political culture was brought to the New England states by the Puritans and was reenforced by the Scandinavians and other northern Europeans. It is characterized by an emphasis on the commonwealth rather than the individual. Government is seen as a means to achieve the public good through positive action, and although nongovernmental activity is preferred, governmental activity is considered appropriate when it enhances the community. Public service is every citizen's responsibility, which tends to give rise to amateur or part-time politicians.

The individualistic political culture came to America by way of groups from non-Puritan England and the interior Germanic states who were from very different ethnic and religious backgrounds than their moralistic counterparts. They settled primarily the middle parts of the nation. Individual opportunity in a pluralistic society is the emphasis of this culture, and the principal role of government is to maintain a free marketplace where the individual may thrive. Although some enter government "to serve," politics is normally just another means for individuals to improve their social and economic position. This culture tends to foster professional rather than amateur politics; those who participate in politics receive a compensation commensurate with the position, which fosters full-time politicians.

The traditionalistic political culture is "an extension of the landed gentry agrarianism of the Old World" (Elazar 1984, 130), and in America it developed primarily in the southern states. Government has a positive role in the community, but this role is one of maintaining and supporting the existing order. In essence, it promotes the private good of the existing elite. The political system is undergirded by a fine web of informal personal relationships that develop over the years and that substitute for a more formal bureaucracy. The appropriate elite governs, and political office is often "inherited" through family or social ties (Elazar 1984, 119).

As a system of ideal types or a model, the typology

developed by Elazar is very helpful in understanding the concept of political culture. His attempt to place states or sections of states in one or more of the subcultures is interesting, but it has been criticized as "more impressionistic than systematic" (Jewell and Olson 1982, 8), a criticism that is supported by the general lack of systematic state data in Elazar's work. Nonetheless, his typology is a place to start as we attempt to understand the political culture of Iowa. He classifies Iowa as a moralistic-individualistic political culture; that is, the moralistic culture dominates, but there is also a strong individualistic strain (Elazar 1984, 136).

Iowa's Political Culture

As a first attempt to understand the political culture of Iowa, we examine Iowans' attitudes toward government and its role. Although systematic data on the subject are not voluminous, there is sufficient evidence to form some generalizations. Recent poll data indicate that Iowans consider themselves very patriotic. Responding to the question "How patriotic do you consider yourself—very patriotic, somewhat patriotic or not patriotic at all?" over half of the voting-age population (60%) said they are very patriotic, over one-third (38%) are somewhat patriotic, and a small fraction (2%) indicated they are not at all patriotic (*Iowa Poll: 1984*, poll no. 1156).

The people of Iowa also have very positive feelings about their state. A poll conducted in March 1982 indicated that even though they had just endured one of the worst winters in history, two-thirds (69%) would prefer to live in Iowa rather than in another state. Apparently aware that the sun does shine more warmly on other places, a minority of the over-eighteen population (29%) would prefer to live elsewhere, and the top five alternatives were states in the Sun Belt (*Iowa Poll: 1982*, poll no. 1050).

The very positive feelings held by Iowa citizens about their nation and state do not, however, necessarily translate into strong support for the activities and personnel of government. The Iowa political culture fosters the idea of limited government. Private, nongovernment activity is preferred, and government activities and politicians are viewed with some suspicion. Only about a third of the state's voting-age population (34%) believe that "most political office-holders generally tell the public the truth," while a majority (59%) think that "politicians are generally untruthful" (*Iowa Poll: 1982*, poll no. 1054). Perhaps because they are suspicious of politicians and government activity in general, Iowans have long supported a merit-based state civil service rather than a system of appointments based on political patronage.

The major focus of the 1986 session of the general assembly was the reorganization and "downsizing" of Iowa state government, which politicians and citizens alike perceived as having grown too large. In one poll, almost three times as many Iowans supported as opposed Governor Terry Branstad's proposal to reorganize state government (49% to 18%, with 33% undecided). The same poll indicated that nearly half of Iowa's citizens (46%) thought that the state had too many employees, while one in five considered employment levels to be "about right" (21%) and one in ten believed that the state had too few employees (11%). Moreover, it is interesting that although the governor attempted to sell government reorganization as an economy move, few citizens (27%) believed the action would decrease the size of the state budget; the largest group (37%) thought that it would make no difference or would even increase the state budget somewhat (16%) (*Iowa Poll: 1986*, poll no. 1251). It seems likely that a belief in lean and limited government rather than bugetary savings was the basis for citizen support of a reorganized and smaller state government. (The general assembly overwhelmingly approved the reorganization plan, which reduced the size of state government and gave the governor more direct control of the executive branch.)

Institutions generally fare better with the citizens of Iowa than do the activities and personnel of government. Iowans have been asked on several occasions (most recently in 1981) to express their confidence in a number of government, business, and social institutions, and in general they have expressed confidence in government institutions. They regarded federal, state, and local institutions as more trustworthy in 1981 than in 1977 (the last time the question was asked), and, indeed, Iowans on the average have more confidence in public than in business institutions (*Iowa Poll: 1981*, poll no. 1022). Finally, although there is much disagreement about specific policy actions, citizens generally approve of the way the Iowa General Assembly handles legislative sessions. In 1984 half (50%) approved of the outcome of the legislative session, while less than a third (29%) disapproved, with the remainder (21%) holding no opinion (unpublished Iowa Poll 1984). The 1984 attitudes toward the legislature were virtually the same as those produced by a 1977 Iowa poll.

Government activity tends to be limited to areas that cannot be undertaken conveniently by private-sector institutions or individual citizens themselves. Beyond the areas of public education (which received about 55 percent of the appropriations from the General Fund in the 1985 through 1987 fiscal years) and the construction and maintenance of roads and highways (about 90 percent of 1985–87 non–General Fund appropriations), there is little consensus among Iowans as to what properly constitutes a public issue. In recent years there has been a general acceptance of the Great Society social welfare programs (about 17 to 18 percent of 1985–87 General Fund appropriations), but the work ethic and individual self-reliance are still firmly entrenched in the Iowa political culture.

Public service is viewed as the duty of citizens, and this results in part-time, or citizen, politics. Those who serve in elected or appointed political positions generally receive little or no remuneration for their public service. Members of state boards and commissions, city councils, and local boards and commissions, as well as most mayors, are amateur officials who donate their time to the public. Members of the state legislature are also part-time (1986 legislative salaries were $14,600 plus travel and per diem allowances), and, with some exceptions, they depend on other jobs or professions for most of their income. There continues to be a very strong bias against political office as a full-time endeavor, which in Iowa is seen as synonymous with big government and a loss of citizen control.

Those who pursue public service are expected to serve honestly and in the public interest. Although government service is fraught with potential conflicts of interest, the slightest indiscretion can be very costly in Iowa. For example, a recent Speaker of the Iowa House of Representatives lost his leadership position, and ultimately his seat in the general assembly, for claiming homestead exemptions for the property taxes on both his Des Moines and district homes in violation of state law, which permits the exemption to be taken on only a single residence (Bullard 1979, 3A). Similarly, the internal rules of the Iowa General Assembly require lobbyists, legislators, and their employees to report gifts or expenditures in excess of fifteen dollars (gifts of fifty dollars or more are prohibited), and these are periodically published by local newspapers.

The nature of political competition in Iowa has also been influenced by the political culture, which emphasizes issues and public concerns rather than individual loyalties and partisan friendships. Nonpartisan elections are common at the local government level, and although political parties are well developed in the state, they tend not to be valued for their own sake. Iowans have demonstrated a strong propensity for political independence; in 1986 33.5 percent of those registered to vote claimed no party identification. There is widespread split-ticket voting, and Iowa has a history of volatility in its support for Republicans and Democrats in elections. Examples are numerous. In 1986 Senator Charles Grassley was the first U.S. senator from Iowa to be reelected in twenty years, and the other U.S. senator is a Democrat. Of the six U.S. representatives, four are Republicans and two are Democrats. The Republican governor, Terry Branstad, was reelected in 1986, but five of the other six elective state executive offices went to Democrats. There are presently only two major parties in Iowa, though in the past, several minor parties—including the Anti-Monopoly, Greenback, Populist, and Prohibition parties—have qualified as political parties (Ross 1957, 28–29). Neither the existence of minor parties in the past, however, nor the current trend toward nonpartisan elections, large numbers of independent voters, split-ticket voting, and electoral volatility belies the fact that the political party system in Iowa has grown stronger and increasingly competitive in recent years. This fact is largely attributable to increased urbanization and perhaps the increased influence of individualistic elements in the political culture.

Both major parties are organized hierarchically from the local to the state level. To conduct party business, they use a caucus and convention system that does not differ greatly from that found in other states. The local caucuses elect delegates to county conventions, which in turn elect delegates to district and state conventions, where the delegates to the national conventions are selected. Typically it is the party activists who are the glue that binds this system together, serving as unpaid officials at each level of activity. But in recent presidential campaigns, the publicity associated with the precinct caucuses has drawn many "political amateurs" into the process. A recent fifty-state study of the organizational strength of local party systems ranked Iowa Republicans and Democrats seventeenth and twenty-seventh respectively (Gibson et al. 1985, 154–55). The data are for 1964 through 1979, however, so they do not reflect the 1980 and 1984 caucuses, which have

greatly stimulated activity in Iowa and may have strengthened organization at the local level in both parties.

The system relies on volunteer assistance at all levels,
but at the state level in Des Moines, both parties have a
well-developed organization with a party headquarters and
a paid professional staff. The state party organizations play
a significant role in fund-raising, the identification and registration of party supporters, the recruitment of candidates, and a variety of campaign activities in election
years.

Students of state politics have shown a great interest
in two-party competition, which is highly valued in the
United States. Although there is disagreement about the
impact of interparty competition on the policy process,
and the democratic process itself, Murray S. Stedman, Jr.,
maintains that "most political scientists who study party
systems remain convinced that interparty competition
strongly affects the organization and activities of the parties" (1976, 75). Historically, only about half of the states
have been classified as competitive two-party systems, and
this remains the case. Since the New Deal party realignment of the 1930s, however, there have been significant
changes in the competitive patterns of state party systems,
with many more states now classified under Austin Ranney's system of classification as "modified one-party Democratic" and far fewer falling into the "modified one-party
Republican" category (Bibby et al. 1983, 66).

The Iowa party system, once classified as "modified
one-party Republican" (Ranney 1965, 65), is now one of
twenty-two states classified as "two-party competitive,"
and in fact during the period from 1974 to 1980 Iowa was
the seventh most competitive of the fifty state party systems (Bibby et al. 1983, 66). This represents a dramatic
change from the earlier Republican dominance in Iowa. Of
the seventy-two terms of the Iowa General Assembly from
1846 through 1988, Republicans controlled the senate
fifty-eight times and the house sixty-one, but Democrats

have elected a majority in both houses in five of the last seven legislatures. Republicans continue to dominate in gubernatorial races (winning eight of the eleven contests from 1960 to 1986 and seven in a row, from 1968 to 1986) although they carried only 52 percent of the vote in the very competitive 1986 gubernatorial election. Additionally, the candidate in five of the seven most recent Republican victories was the very popular Robert Ray, who won the support of many Democrats (Stork and Clingan 1980, 5–8; *Iowa Official Register 1985-86*, 203–5). Increased urbanization and industrialization have brought more blue-collar employees into the work force, and when combined with traditional religious and ethnic bases, they probably account for much of the growth in Democratic strength in Iowa. The Democratic party is particularly strong in the southeastern counties, in the larger urban areas, and in counties with large Catholic populations. (Democrats enjoy a slight advantage in registered voters; at the time of the 1986 elections, 35.3 percent were listed as Democrats, 31.2 percent as Republicans, and 33.5 percent as "no party.")

Elazar asserts that citizen participation (as demonstrated by voter turnout) is associated with political culture and that states with moralistic political cultures have higher turnout levels than individualistic states, which in turn have greater participation than states with traditional cultures (Elazar 1984, 152). Iowans apparently do have a great deal of faith in the efficacy of electoral politics. In terms of the percentage of the voting-age population registered to vote, Iowa ranked tenth in 1980 with 83.5 percent of the eligible voters registered, compared to 70.4 percent nationwide. Iowa consistently ranks high among the states (eighth in 1972 and 1976, ninth in 1980, eighth again in 1984) in terms of the percentage of the voting-age population casting votes in presidential elections. In 1984, 62.3 percent of those eligible voted in the presidential race, compared to 53.3 percent nationally; in 1980 the Iowa and national figures were 63 and 52.6 percent; in 1976 they were 63.1 and 53.5, and in 1972 64 and 55.2 percent (*Statistical Abstract of the United States: 1986*, 255).

The high levels of voter registration and participation in presidential elections are evidence that Iowans have strong feelings of citizen duty. On indices of citizen participation, Iowa consistently ranks high among the fifty states, which is further evidence of the strong moralistic influence in the state's political culture.

Iowa's Demographics

A major determinant of political culture is the demographic composition of the population. After growing steadily but undramatically from 1910 to 1980, the population of Iowa declined in the first half of the 1980s. The 1985 Bureau of the Census estimate of 2,884,000 for the Iowa population represents a 1 percent decline from the 1980 figure of 2,913,808. Modest growth in recent decades has resulted in a decline in Iowa's ranking among the fifty states from its position as the twentieth most populous state in 1940 to twenty-ninth in 1985 (except where noted, demographic data are from the *Statistical Abstract of the United States: 1986*, 1–52).

Census data also indicate a continuation of the trend toward urbanization in Iowa, with 59 percent of the people residing in urban areas and 41 percent in rural areas. The urban population of Iowa exceeded the rural population for the first time in 1960. The census bureau definition of an urban area (a population of at least 2,500) is very liberal, however, and Iowa is clearly a state of small communities: only 123 of the 955 municipalities qualified as urban areas in 1982, 17 exceeded 25,000 persons, 3 had more than 100,000, and this includes Des Moines, the state's largest city, with fewer than 200,000 residents (*Statistical Profile of Iowa: 1985,* 72, 76). Further evidence of the small-town nature of Iowa is provided by the fact that only 40 percent of the population resides in a Standard Metropolitan Statistical Area (SMSA), compared to 75 percent nationwide. (An SMSA is a large population nucleus—an urban area of 50,000 or more—and any adjacent communities that are economically and socially integrated with the nucleus.)

The Iowa population is becoming increasingly homogenized as national origins grow less distinct. Over half (55%) of Iowans claimed multiple ancestry or did not specify ancestry in the 1980 census. Still, many groups in Iowa identify with and retain Old World customs. Germans represent the largest ancestral group (21% in 1980), followed by those of an English or Irish background (7% and 4% respectively).

The population of Iowa is 97.4 percent white. Blacks constitute only 1.4 percent of the state's population, and two-thirds of Iowa's black residents live in Des Moines, Waterloo, and Davenport, leaving many areas of the state with few or no black residents. Other nonwhite groups, such as Asians and American Indians, made up the remaining 1.2 percent of the state's population as of 1980.

Iowa also has other distinctive demographic characteristics. Three-fifths of Iowa's population (61.2%) claim religious affiliation, compared to about half (49.7%) of the national population. Roman Catholics, Lutherans, and Methodists make up the three largest denominations found in the state, with Methodists strong in most of Iowa's ninety-nine counties. The number of women residents of Iowa exceeded that of men for the first time in the 1950 census (Ross 1957, 6–7), and women now represent 51.4 percent of the population, which compares favorably with the national figure (*Statistical Profile of Iowa: 1985,* 73). Finally, Iowa has an aging population. Young people leaving the state have contributed to a disproportionately large number of citizens aged sixty-five and over (13.8 percent in Iowa, compared to 11.3 percent nationwide).

The Demographics of Iowa's Politics

Iowa does appear to include many of the demographic and political characteristics of the moralistic-individualistic political culture outlined by Elazar. Although increasingly homogenized, the ethnic and religious backgrounds of most Iowans are heavily tilted toward England and northern Europe. The small-town nature of the state, the fact that many rural residents remain tied to the land, and the problem of a lack of major in-migration combined with significant out-migration by young Iowans have all contributed to a stable but older population that has not changed dramatically. The continuing urbanization has made Iowa a more pluralistic culture (although the dominant factor remains the urban-rural split), and urbanization has probably moved the political culture somewhat in the direction of individualism.

Iowans view government with some suspicion and prefer that it be limited to activities not conveniently carried out by the private sector. They like small, efficient governments staffed by citizens who donate, or virtually donate, their time for the good of the community. When government activity requires full-time employees, professionals are sought to work within the state's strong civil service system.

A strong sense of citizen duty has promoted a high level of political participation, with Iowa consistently ranking in the top 20 percent of the states in terms of voter registration and participation in elections. The combination of a sense of citizen duty and a skepticism about government and professional politicians, particularly in rural areas, has maintained the citizen or amateur nature of Iowa politics. The state is also well known for its clean politics. Those who serve the public are judged by very high ethical standards, which certainly reflects the moralistic, as opposed to the individualistic, dimension of the political culture.

The political party system has evolved from a Republican-dominated one into a highly competitive two-party system. Although the party system is growing stronger, particularly at the state and county levels, there remains a high degree of political independence among state voters.

Iowa is a small, agriculturally oriented state in the American heartland. The people are moralistic, traditional, and moderate. To suggest, however, that a state with virtually no major urban centers, few big labor unions, and a very small minority population is representative of the traditionally Democratic states or a microcosm of the national Democratic party stretches the imagination. Although more representative of the Republican party, Iowa is simply too small to play such a large role in the nomination of Republican presidential candidates; perhaps no state should be a presidential kingmaker. Moreover, the rural, midwestern nature of Iowa is advantageous to some candidates—McGovern and Mondale were well-known neighbors; Reagan lived and worked in the state; Carter had a small-town, rural background—and disadvantageous to others, those who do not fit the Iowa mold. Iowa may well mislead the nation about the political appeal of presidential candidates.

References

Bibby, John F., Cornelius P. Cotter, James L. Gibson, and Robert J. Huckshorn. 1983. "Parties in State Politics." In *Politics in the American States*, 4th ed., edited by Virginia Gray, Herbert Jacob, and Kenneth N. Vines, 59–96. Boston: Little, Brown.

Bullard, Charles. 1979. "Dual Tax-Credit Filing a 'Mistake,' Mullin Says." *Des Moines Register*, December 19, p. 3A.

Des Moines Register. 1986.

Elazar, Daniel J. 1984. *American Federalism: A View from the States*. 3d ed. New York: Harper and Row.

Gibson, James L., Cornelius P. Cotter, John F. Bibby, and Robert

J. Huckshorn. 1985. "Whither the Local Parties? A Cross-Sectional and Longitudinal Analysis of the Strength of Party Organizations." *American Journal of Political Science* 29: 139–60.

Hahn, Harlan. 1971. *Urban-Rural Conflict*. Beverly Hills, Calif.: Sage.

Iowa Official Register: 1965–66. 1965. Des Moines: State of Iowa.

Iowa Official Register: 1985–86. 1985. Des Moines: State of Iowa.

The Iowa Poll. 1983–87. Vols. for 1982 through 1986. Des Moines: Des Moines Register and Tribune Company.

Jewell, Malcolm E., and David M. Olson. 1982. *American State Political Parties and Elections*. Rev. ed. Homewood, Ill.: Dorsey.

Patterson, Samuel C. 1968. "The Political Cultures of American States." *Journal of Politics* 30: 187–209.

Ranney, Austin. 1965. "Parties and State Politics." In *Politics in the American States*, edited by Herbert Jacob and Kenneth Vines, 61–99. Boston: Little, Brown.

Ross, Russell M. 1957. *The Government and Administration of Iowa*. New York: Thomas Y. Crowell.

Statistical Abstract of the United States: 1986. 1985. Prepared by the Bureau of the Census. Washington, D.C.: Government Printing Office.

Statistical Profile of Iowa: 1985. 1985. Des Moines: Iowa Development Commission.

Stedman, Murray S., Jr. 1976. *State and Local Governments*. Cambridge, Mass.: Winthrop.

Stork, Frank J. 1980. *Lawmaking in Iowa*. Des Moines: Iowa Senate.

Stork, Frank J., and Cynthia A. Clingan. 1980. *The Iowa General Assembly: Our Legislative Heritage, 1846–1980*. Des Moines: Iowa Senate.

★★★★★ **3** ★★★★★★★★★★

The Iowa Precinct Caucuses: The Decades of Obscurity

The caucus system is a product of the Jacksonian democracy of the early 1830s. To that time, the dominant system for nominating public officials in the United States had been one of caucuses by members of Congress and the state legislatures, but the new system began with precinct caucuses that were, theoretically at least, open to all party members. The local caucuses were to elect delegates to county conventions, and from there the system proceeded through district, state, and national conventions, just as today. In practice, however, since it was not regulated by government, the caucus system came to be dominated by party bosses in the latter half of the nineteenth century (Crotty and Jackson 1985, chap. 1), and it was not until the Progressive era in the first two decades of the twentieth century that the various state legislatures brought the system under the rule of law.

Developments through 1917

When Iowa joined the Union in 1846, the state's political parties immediately adopted the caucus

Portions of this chapter were published as "The Evolution of the Iowa Precinct Caucuses," in the *Annals of Iowa* 47 (Spring 1983): 618–35. Used by permission of the Iowa State Historical Department.

and convention system. As in other states, charges of manipulation and foul play soon emerged. Emory English, in an article on voting practices in Iowa, outlined a number of common caucus abuses. Generally, cliques or special-interest groups dominated party organizations and did their best to limit participation by opposing factions or the general public. Often the times and locations of caucuses were closely guarded secrets, and "snap" caucuses were a favorite device of those "in the know." The knowledgeable would assemble on short notice, elect a slate of delegates to the county convention, and quickly adjourn. When outsiders became aware of caucus times in advance, a caucus might be packed with the supporters of a particular candidate or slate of delegates, or a "competing event" might be organized. English recounts an example of a "competing event" held in northern Iowa in which "the 'fortunate' burning of an old shed in the outskirts of a small town at exactly the advertised hour . . . of the caucus attracted nine-tenths of the people of the village, including members of the volunteer fire department. In the meantime, those in the 'know' assembled at the caucus, . . . selected a 'slate' of delegates without opposition and adjourned" (English 1948, 257).

Frequent abuses of the caucus process led to calls for reform, but the Iowa General Assembly was slow to act; the first reform bill was not introduced until 1896. Progressive era reformers focused on developing a system of primary elections in Iowa rather than on taking the less radical step of revising the caucus and convention system. Three reform bills were introduced and rejected by the Twenty-sixth General Assembly in 1896 (Crossley 1903, 174–75), but in 1898 the Twenty-seventh General Assembly enacted a primary election law for Iowa's counties, though it did not make the primary system compulsory (Ia. Gen. Assem. 1898, chap. 111, p. 59). The first compulsory primary election law passed the Thirtieth General Assembly in 1904, but it applied only to counties with populations in excess of 75,000, and Polk was the only county affected (Ia. Gen. Assem. 1904, chap. 40, p. 29).

In 1907 eleven years of reform efforts in the general assembly culminated in the passage of a statewide primary election law. The law provided for primary elections to nominate candidates for any office filled by direct popular vote in the general election, with the exception of judgeships. It also required that delegates to the county conventions, members of the county central committees, and presidential and vice-presidential electors be nominated by primary election. Finally, it required a preference poll for United States senators, who at that time were chosen by the state legislature. Since the 1907 law only affected offices filled by direct popular vote, it did not provide for the nomination of presidential candidates. Moreover, the district and state conventions, not a popular vote, still selected delegates to the national conventions. The 1907 law, however, did represent a major change in Iowa electoral politics, since it opened the previously closed party system to the voters and limited the parties' control over the nominating process (Ia. Gen. Assem. 1907, chap. 51, p. 51).

Although amended several times, the 1907 law remained substantially intact until 1963. Changes in 1913 and 1917 are, however, worthy of examination. In those years Iowa initiated and then abolished a presidential primary. In 1913 the Thirty-fifth General Assembly amended Iowa's primary election law to include the selection of delegates and alternate delegates to the national conventions of all political parties, the selection of national committee members for each party, and a presidential preference poll "for the purpose of ascertaining the sentiment of voters of the state in the respective parties as to candidates for president and vice-president of the United States" (Ia. Gen. Assem. 1913, chap. 111, p. 99).

Iowa held its only presidential primary election on April 10, 1916, with mixed results. None of the major presidential candidates entered the primary (Schier 1980, 58 n. 49), less than one-third of the eligible electorate voted, and the primary election cost the state $122,000 (*Des Moines Register* Jan. 30, 1917, 2; hereafter cited as *DMR*). Governor George W. Clarke, who in his inaugural address of January 16, 1913, had called for the passage of a presidential preference primary law (Clarke 1913, 19–20), now branded the 1916 presidential preference poll a "farce." In his final biennial message to the general assembly in 1917, he urged the repeal of the entire direct primary law and called for the return to the caucus and convention system of selecting candidates for public office (Clarke 1917, 27).

The Thirty-seventh General Assembly was not willing to abolish the direct primary law in its entirety, but it did agree with Governor Clarke's assessment of the presidential preference primary. A bill to repeal this section unanimously passed both houses in early 1917, and the newly inaugurated governor, William L. Harding, ended Iowa's short flirtation with the presidential primary by signing it into law on February 16, 1917 (Ia. Gen. Assem. 1917, chap. 14, p. 32). Thus, with the one exception in 1916, Iowa has employed the caucus and convention system to select presidential delegates to national conventions.

The Modern Caucus System

The next major modification of the caucus and convention system occurred in 1963, when the general assembly amended Iowa's primary election law and returned the selection of county convention delegates to the precinct caucuses (Ia. Gen. Assem. 1963, chap. 78, p. 117). Two years later, lawmakers also removed the selection of county committee members from electoral politics and provided for their selection at the precinct caucuses (Ia. Gen. Assem. 1965, chap. 89, p. 158). Several factors contributed to these changes, including the high cost of printing separate ballots for each precinct, the low visibility of party offices, and a movement in Iowa for a shorter ballot (Larson 1981). No additional substantive changes in the Iowa primary law occurred after 1965. The current law requires primary elections to nominate candidates for all elective offices below that of president with the exception of judgeships and provides for a caucus and convention system for selecting delegates to the national conventions.

When the general assembly returned Iowa to the caucus and convention system for selecting delegates and committee members, it regulated their conduct. Iowa law provides that "delegates to county conventions of political parties and party committee members shall be elected at precinct caucuses held not later than the fourth Monday in February on each even-numbered year. The date shall be at least eight days earlier than the scheduled date for any meeting, caucus or primary which constitutes the first determining stage of the presidential nominating process in any other state" (Iowa, *Code: 1985*, sec. 43.4). This section of the code has been amended several times, most recently in 1983, with the legislative intent to preserve Iowa's first-in-the-nation status, and these efforts are the subject of a later chapter (Ia. Gen. Assem. 1983, chap. 138, p. 306).

The actual date for precinct caucuses is set by the state central committee of each party, and since 1976 the Republican and Democratic parties have held their caucuses on the same day. The principal motivation for this unusual example of party cooperation in Iowa is to gain maximum media exposure, and in that they have succeeded. (Tim Hyde, former executive director of the Iowa Republican party, listed two additional reasons for the Republicans' willingness to initiate a common caucus date: to maximize caucus participation through joint announcements and to prevent people from participating in both the Republican and Democratic caucuses [1982].) The state central committee determines a uniform starting time for all Democratic caucuses. The county central committees control the starting time for Republican caucuses in each county, which results in some variation in the evening starting times. Iowa law also requires that "the date, time, and place of each precinct caucus of a political party shall be published at least twice . . . not more than thirty days and not less than five days before the date of the caucuses." In addition, the notice must state in substance that each voter affiliated with the specified political party may attend the precinct caucus (Iowa, *Code: 1985*, sec. 43.92). Finally, whenever possible, precinct caucuses are to be held in publicly owned buildings or in places used for holding public meetings (Iowa, *Code: 1985*, sec. 43.93). These requirements are intended to ensure an open and well-publicized caucus process and have succeeded in eliminating most of the earlier abuses. It is still possible to pack a caucus with supporters of a particular candidate or slate of delegates, but greater media coverage and the correspondingly higher salience of the caucuses make the use of this tactic increasingly difficult, especially in presidential election years.

The legislation of 1965 also determined the rules of eligibility for caucus participation. The law requires that caucus participants reside within the precinct and that they are or will be eligible electors by the next general election. The law permits seventeen-year-olds who will be eighteen by the time of the general election to participate in the caucuses (Iowa, *Code: 1985*, sec. 43.90). Since the precinct caucuses are party-sponsored events, the parties may have, and each has, additional requirements for participation. Neither party requires that participants be registered to vote, but the Iowa Republican party requires that "any person voting at a precinct caucus must be a Republican" and authorizes the resolution of eligibility disputes by majority vote of the caucus (Republican Party of Iowa 1984, p. 4). The Democratic party limits participation to those who "support the purpose of the Democratic party, and who are registered Democrats, or who register at the time of their request to participate" in the caucuses (Iowa Democratic Party 1984a, p. 1). Although the goal of these requirements is to prevent raiding by the opposition, it is very unlikely that persons willing to "declare" themselves supporters of the party on the evening of the caucus will be prevented from participating by either the Republicans or the Democrats.

Voting procedures within caucuses are at the discretion of each caucus gathering, although the Republican state central committee suggests that votes be taken by secret ballot. Moreover, any questions not covered by state law or party rules are resolved by majority vote of the caucus participants.

The principal concerns of the precinct caucuses are the selection of delegates and the development of issues for the party platform, but the parties vary somewhat in their conduct of business. Both normally elect two precinct committee members to represent their precinct on the county central committee. Each begins the platform-building process by developing and discussing issues, which are then forwarded to the county platform committee. Republican caucuses "take stands" and Democrats "prioritize" the issues. The Democratic caucuses elect members and alternates to serve on the platform committee and the committee on committees, which plan the county conventions. The Republican county committees determine the procedures for filling these positions, and the procedures vary by county.

Iowa as the First Nominating Event

From a position of relative obscurity, the Iowa precinct caucuses moved toward national prominence in 1972, when the Iowa Democratic party moved its caucus date forward to January 24, making it the first primary event in the nation. The early date for the caucuses is the result of an interesting series of events. The Iowa General Assembly first passed legislation governing the date of precinct caucuses in 1969. The law required that caucuses be held "not later than the second Monday in May in each election year" but did not limit how early they might be held (Ia. Gen. Assem. 1969, chap. 90, p. 124). Prior to 1972 the Iowa political parties tended to hold their precinct caucuses in late March or in April, which fell in the middle of the national primary schedule.

The earlier date was prompted by reforms in the caucus and convention system adopted by the Iowa Democrats between 1968 and 1972. Foremost among the changes was the decision to hold separate district and state conventions and to require proportional representation in the delegate selection process. To facilitate the implementation of the reforms, the Democrats added a clause to their party constitution requiring thirty days between party functions (precinct caucuses, county conventions, congressional district conventions, the state statutory convention, the state presidential convention, and the national convention). Due to the decision to hold the Democratic state convention on May 20—a decision based largely on the availability of a suitable meeting place—the latest possible date for the caucuses in 1972 was January 24 (Larson 1983). The January date moved the Iowa Democratic caucuses ahead of the New Hampshire primary election, which was traditionally the nation's first primary event.

The clause in the Democratic party's constitution requiring thirty days between events arose from practical rather than philosophical considerations. The party wanted both to include as many Democrats as possible in the caucus process and to provide delegates to the next set of party functions with good sources of information. Unfortunately, the state party headquarters had severe physical limitations and very poor office equipment, so to complete the paperwork and arrangements required for each level of meetings, a one-month interlude between party functions was necessary. Party leaders maintain that there was no political intent in moving the caucus date forward and confess that they were unaware that the Iowa Democratic caucuses would be the nation's first as a result of the

The Iowa precinct caucuses were inconspicuous events prior to 1972. The strictly local functions, held in the middle of the primary and caucus season, were the first step in the process of selecting delegates to the national conventions. The Iowa parties' caucus and convention process rarely received national media attention since they elected less than 2 percent of the delegates to their respective national conventions. When the Iowa Democrats chose an earlier date for their caucuses, the national parties and the media quickly took notice.

move. It did not take Iowa Democrats long, however, to realize what they had done, and although surprised by the media attention, they set out to capitalize on their new position of prominence (Larson 1983).

References

Clarke, George W. 1913. *Iowa Documents*. Inaugural Address to the Thirty-fifth General Assembly, January 16.

_____. 1917. *Iowa Documents*. Biennial Message to the Thirty-seventh General Assembly, January 9.

Crossley, James J. 1903. "The Regulation of Primary Elections by Law." *Iowa Journal of History and Politics* 1: 165–92.

Crotty, William, and John S. Jackson III. 1985. *Presidential Primaries and Nominations*. Washington, D.C.: CQ Press.

Des Moines Register. 1917.

English, Emory H. 1948. "Evolution in Iowa Voting Practices." *Annals of Iowa* 29: 249–89.

Hyde, Tim. 1982. Telephone interview with author, October 8. Hyde was the executive director of the Iowa Republican party from 1980 to 1983.

Iowa. 1985. *Code of Iowa: 1985*.

Iowa Democratic Party. 1980. Precinct Caucus Kit, 1980. Mimeographed.

_____. 1984a. Constitution. Amended 1984.

_____. 1984b. Precinct Caucus Kit. Mimeographed.

Iowa. General Assembly. 1898–1983. *Acts and Resolutions*. Des Moines: State of Iowa.

Larson, Clifton. 1981. Telephone interview with author, February 23. Larson was the chair of the Iowa Democratic party from 1970 to 1973.

_____. 1983. Telephone interview with author, March 27.

Republican Party of Iowa. 1980. Suggested Procedure for Precinct Caucuses, January 21, 1980. Mimeographed.

_____. 1983. Conducting Your Precinct Caucus. Mimeographed.

_____. 1984. Constitution. Amended 1984.

Schier, Steven E. 1980. *The Rules of the Game: Democratic National Convention Delegate Selection in Iowa and Wisconsin*. Washington, D.C.: University Press of America.

★★★★★ **4** ★★★★★★★★★

The 1968 and 1972 Caucuses: The Emergence of a National Event

The early date for the precinct caucuses was destined to change their character completely. Before 1972 they were strictly local events; attendance was limited and activism was confined to a small band of partisans whose interest allowed them to dominate the meetings by default. A spirited presidential-nominating contest—the 1952 Eisenhower-Taft race, for example (Clifton 1952, 1)— or a controversial issue—like the 1968 antiwar struggle— increased caucus participation, but this went largely unnoticed at the national level. It is not surprising that the local meetings attracted little national media attention, because Iowa Republicans and Democrats held their caucuses in the middle of the presidential nominating process and selected less than 2 percent of the delegates to their respective national conventions. Thus, even though the meetings were open and were regularly covered by the Iowa news media, they were often poorly attended and of little or no national significance.

The 1968 Precinct Caucuses

Before turning to the events of 1972 that focused national attention on the state, it would be helpful to examine briefly the 1968 precinct caucuses in order to appreciate their purpose and the changes necessary to turn them into a media event. Procedurally, 1968 was a typical year for the caucuses, although the antiwar movement stimulated greater-than-usual participation in the Democratic sessions. Both parties held their 1968 precinct caucuses in March.

The Republican Caucuses. Most of the Republican local meetings in the state's 2484 precincts were held on March 4, and a few on the fifth. The opening round in the contest for Iowa's twenty-four delegates to the national convention in Miami centered around the candidacies of former vice-president Richard Nixon and New York governor Nelson Rockefeller, but there was also interest in some precincts in the possible candidacy of California governor Ronald Reagan (Mills 1968a).

Generally, the sessions went smoothly and according to traditional procedures. After electing local party officials and considering resolutions that might be appropriate for planks in the county platforms, many caucuses conducted a straw poll; others simply elected delegates to county conventions and forwarded their names to state party headquarters over the next several days (*DMR* March 5, 1968, 1, 6). There was no statewide poll or reporting system, and the state party made no systematic attempt to determine the candidate preferences of the delegates elected to the county conventions. In fact, it was not customary for those seeking to represent the precinct at succeeding levels to declare their presidential loyalties, although there were periodic attempts by candidate organizations to require disclosure (*DMR* April 11, 1968, 4). Even when preferences were known, delegates could change their loyalties, since they were not bound to candidates by law. Thus in 1968 Iowa Republicans had no systematic way to determine which candidates had won, or even to judge with any certainty the number of participants in their caucus process.

Local newspapers, however, attempted to provide in-

formation about the candidate preference of caucus participants by covering selected precincts. The *Des Moines
Register*, for example, published information about several
Polk County meetings, noting that "attendance was
spotty," ranging from heavy attendance in some larger precincts to just three persons in a combined caucus of precincts 27, 34, 36, and 37. The paper reported partial results of straw polls taken in Polk County (with Rockefeller
favored by 344 participants, Nixon by 321, and Reagan by
64) and listed some of the resolutions passed in the precinct meetings (*DMR* March 5, 1968, 1, 6). The national
media paid no attention to the Iowa Republican precinct
caucuses.

The local nature of the process and the almost complete absence of systematic information about the candidate preference of caucus participants is further illustrated
by a *Register* editorial shortly after the meetings which
concluded that "Republican precinct caucuses in Iowa last
week showed no clear trend for either of the major presidential prospects. Figures on straw polls (where taken) and
elected county delegates who declared themselves (most
didn't) are so scattered that nobody can read too much into
them" (*DMR* March 12, 1968, 6).

The Democratic Caucuses. The Iowa
Democrats held their 1968 precinct caucuses on March 25,
their county conventions on April 19, and their combined
district and state conventions on May 24 and 25. The Vietnam War was the dominant concern within the Iowa Democratic party, and, as in the rest of the country, it proved a
very divisive issue. The presidential contenders in 1968
were President Lyndon Johnson, whose Vietnam policies
led some Iowa Democrats to fear that he could not carry
the state in November; Senator Eugene McCarthy, with his
potent college cadre of antiwar activists; and Senator Robert Kennedy, who entered the presidential race on March
16, only nine days before the caucuses (Mills 1968b, 1, 3).

Supporters of McCarthy's antiwar campaign spent months organizing at the grass-roots level in an effort to have an impact in Iowa, and in the process they stimulated local interest in the precinct caucuses. The McCarthy campaign attracted many political neophytes into electoral politics in 1968, and large numbers of individuals attended their first precinct caucuses. The presence of large numbers of political amateurs, many of college age, was not greeted warmly by some party regulars, who had grown used to dominating the caucuses. The political newcomers tended to ignore the time-honored tradition of electing established party workers as delegates to county conventions, and "in some counties intense controversy erupted over the tactics used by the McCarthy forces in electing slates of delegates to the county convention" (Schier 1980, 88). It reached the point that the Democratic state chair sent letters to county chairs suggesting that they look into "irregularities" in caucus participation, a thinly veiled recommendation that they check the residences of McCarthy supporters elected as county delegates (Mills 1968d, 1, 3). State Democratic party rules at the time required a six-month residency in the state, sixty days in the county, and ten days in the precinct. They also required that participants be at least twenty-one years old and that they be people who "considered themselves Democrats at the time" of the caucus. The issue quickly died, however, when Governor Harold Hughes announced, "I welcome anybody into the Iowa Democratic Party" (*DMR* April 5, 1968, 11).

As was the case with the Republicans, the Democrats had no formal system to determine and report the presidential preference of caucus participants, and in fact they lacked the ability to ascertain levels of participation throughout the state. Thus local newspaper accounts were based on a limited number of precincts, most selected for reasons of accessibility. Nonetheless, the *Register* quoted Iowa Democratic chairman Clark Rasmussen's estimate that the caucuses attracted perhaps 75,000 people, which the *Register* called the "greatest outpouring of Democrats in such sessions in the state's history" (Mills 1968c, 1).

The *Register* story, whose headline declared, "Foes Capture Large Share of Delegates," concluded that President Lyndon Johnson was in trouble in Iowa. It declared Senator McCarthy the big winner, and his Iowa campaign manager estimated the McCarthy-Kennedy caucus strength at 40 percent (supporters of the two candidates combined forces in a number of precincts to maximize the anti-Johnson effect) (*DMR* March 27, 1968, 6). As with the Republican caucuses, the national news media showed no interest in the Democratic caucuses, which is not surprising, since the campaign for the presidency was well underway and the Iowa Democrats were just beginning their process of electing forty-six delegates to the national convention in Chicago.

On March 31, only six days after the caucuses, President Johnson shocked the country and his supporters in Iowa when, during a speech to the nation on the progress of the Vietnam War, he announced that he would not campaign for reelection. His embarrassing showing in the New Hampshire primary three weeks earlier, where he had shaded McCarthy by 50 to 41 percent, and declining ratings in national public opinion polls were probably the major factors behind Johnson's decision (Weaver 1968, 1). Since the results were not systematically reported and were not reported at all outside Iowa, the Iowa caucuses certainly played little or no role in the decision, but as a result of it, the contest for the presidency in Iowa was wide open (Seplow 1968, 1).

The Impact of the 1968 Caucuses

The 1968 precinct caucuses of both parties demonstrate the grass-roots nature of the process before Iowa became a media event. Small groups of partisans, usually party regulars and a few other highly motivated citizens, came together every two years to begin the caucus and convention process in the state. The meetings frequently were held in private homes, often those of the precinct chair, and the order of business was standard and usually mundane. The participants elected local party officials, representatives on county committees, and delegates to the county convention; circulated nominating petitions for candidates for local, state, and national offices; and discussed issues of concern to the participants and, in presidential years, potential platform issues and approved resolutions concerning them. The normal attendance at precinct caucuses was small, often so limited in rural areas and small towns that it was not possible to elect full slates of delegates to the county conventions or to fill all the elective local party offices. The 1968 Democratic caucuses demonstrated that controversial issues or candidates could stimulate attendance, but given the more reliable information of recent caucuses (Democratic figures for the huge 1984 media event were 75,000), Clark Rasmussen's estimate of a "record" participation in 1968 of perhaps 75,000 was undoubtedly a gross exaggeration.

The 1968 precinct caucuses also show that neither party's procedures were designed to determine winners and losers at the first stage in the multistage Iowa caucus and convention system. There was no systematic attempt to tabulate levels of support for individual presidential candidates. In fact, seldom was the presidential preference of candidates for the position of delegate to the county convention (and succeeding levels) formally announced. Rather, slates of delegates were elected by majority vote, and those elected typically included experienced party workers and elected officials. At no level in the process were formal declarations of candidate support required, and even when expressed, they did not bind the delegates. The first recorded vote for presidential candidates was the first ballot at the national convention. As the newspaper estimates and speculations following the caucuses showed, it was impossible to determine with any precision the level of citizen participation at the local meetings, let alone the level of candidate support among caucus partici- pants and the delegates elected to the county conventions.

Democratic Party Reforms

The 1968 process also demonstrated that although it was local in nature and without national im- pact, the Iowa caucus and convention system could be spirited and could involve tough political infighting. Just two days after the precinct caucuses, George Mills, a senior political reporter, warned that McCarthy's grass-roots vic- tory "conceivably could be followed by defeats at the state convention" (Mills 1968c, 3), and, indeed, Mills's warning proved prophetic. At the Democratic state convention in May, only five of the forty-six national convention dele- gates went to McCarthy (*DMR* May 28, 1968, 3).

The explanation for the McCarthy decline between the caucuses and the state convention is all too clear to stu- dents of party politics. Forty-two percent of the Iowa dele- gation to the national convention was elected "at large" at the state convention in 1968, and the remainder were elected as representatives of the state's seven congres- sional districts. As the caucus and convention process con- tinued, county chairs and other party workers played an ever-increasing role. For example, Mills noted that "a county chairman usually appoints the nominating com- mittee to select a slate of delegates to the state conven- tion," and the county chairs generally did not favor McCarthy (Mills 1968c, 3). Thus the early McCarthy success in the precinct caucuses turned into defeat at the hands of the party pros at the state convention. Reflecting on the loss at the state level, McCarthy's Iowa chair, State Senator Harry Beardsley, observed that "essentially we learned that organization is more important than an issue as you move through the party process" (*DMR* May 28, 1968, 3).

Those familiar with the 1968 Democratic National Convention in Chicago will recall that party pros were in control there also. While Mayor Richard J. Daley and the Democratic bosses managed the convention proceedings, the anti–Vietnam War protest movement, which provided the basis for the McCarthy presidential candidacy, was reduced to demonstrating in the streets of Chicago, and they did not fare well there either. Unfortunately for the Democratic party, the American public witnessed from a front-row seat the spectacle of Mayor Daley and the bosses leading their party down the road of political suicide. Television cameras and reporters were everywhere, even in the streets experiencing the tear-gassing with the protesters. The message conveyed by television seemed to be that grass-roots politics was merely an exercise; the real decisions were made by the party pros.

The bad feelings created within the Democratic party by the bitter national convention undoubtedly contributed to the defeat of the party's candidate, Hubert Humphrey, by Vice-President Richard Nixon in the general election. It was not long before calls to reform the party's selection procedures were heard. The party responded by creating the McGovern-Fraser Commission to examine and make recommendations about delegate selection procedures, and the commission's report led to new rules for the 1972 caucus and convention process.

The goal of the new party rules was to expand the influence of the grass-roots levels of the party by limiting the ability of party activists and bosses to work their magic at succeeding levels in the caucus and convention system. The rules replaced the winner-take-all system with one requiring proportional representation at succeeding levels of the delegate selection process. The new guidelines also required that 75 percent of the national convention delegates be chosen at levels no higher than the congressional district convention and called for affirmative action to insure the inclusion of women, minorities, and young people in state delegations (Crotty and Jackson 1985, chap. 2). Theoretically, under the new rules a strong showing at the precinct caucus level would lead to proportional representation at the county and succeeding levels, and this would prevent a recurrence of the 1968 experience of McCarthy's being thwarted by party bosses.

Delegate Selection

The Iowa caucus and convention system does not differ greatly from that found in other states. It begins with precinct caucuses open to all citizens willing to declare themselves supporters of the party whose caucus they attend. Although the precinct caucuses perform several party functions, in presidential years the foremost concern is the election of delegates to county conventions, and Democratic and Republican delegate selection procedures differ significantly. For the Iowa precinct caucuses to become a media event and an integral part of the presidential nominating process, the delegate selection procedures of both parties had to be modified to generate "results" or "outcomes" that would allow the media to determine "winners" and "losers."

Democratic Procedures. In the Democratic party's system of proportional representation, delegates to county conventions are elected in proportion to the level of support for the various presidential candidates in each caucus. There may be, and there usually is, an uncommitted group. Either a candidate preference group or an uncommitted group that includes 15 percent of the total caucus voters is considered viable, meaning that it is eligible to elect delegates to the county convention. If more than 85 percent of those voting at a caucus support one presidential candidate or are uncommitted, they are entitled to elect the entire slate of delegates to the county convention (Iowa Democratic Party 1984a).

Delegate selection in Democratic caucuses is a multistage process, with opportunities for bargaining and politicking at each stage. After the chair determines the number of eligible voting members in attendance, caucus participants divide into presidential preference groups. When that stage is completed, the groups are counted for the purpose of determining viability, and preference groups that fail to meet the minimum viability standard have the opportunity to reassociate with other groups. At this point, politicking increases in intensity as viable groups seek to proselytize the "groupless" voters in order to increase the number of county delegates for which they qualify. When all voters are members of a viable candidate preference group or an uncommitted group, the caucus chair again counts the groups and determines the number of delegates to the county convention that each is entitled to elect. The chair informs the county headquarters of the number of delegates committed to each candidate and the number selected as uncommitted, and the final step of delegate selection begins. Delegate selection within groups is often a lively and spirited process that frequently involves speechmaking, bargaining, and vote trading.

As noted, some of the delegates selected are "committed" to support specific candidates at the county convention; others are elected as uncommitted delegates. Committed delegates, however, are not legally bound to support a particular candidate at the county level, nor are delegates from the county to the state convention so bound (Iowa Democratic Party 1980). Similarly, a Hunt Commission recommendation accepted by the Democratic National Committee at its March 26, 1982, meeting called for the abolition of the practice followed in 1980 of binding state delegates at the national convention.

The system of proportional representation made it possible to translate caucus outcomes into "delegate equivalents" at succeeding steps in the process. Since 1972 state Democratic officials have calculated the percentage of weighted county convention delegates (called "state delegate equivalents") won by each of the presidential candidates at the precinct caucuses. They have also projected "national delegate equivalents," that is, the future delegate strength of presidential candidates within the Iowa delegation to the Democratic National Convention (Bender 1983).

The final step in meeting the media's demand for "outcomes" was taken when the Iowa Democratic party developed a system for compiling caucus results on the evening of the local meetings. In 1972 party officials prepared a list of randomly selected precincts for the purpose of calculating the "state delegate equivalents" and projecting the state delegates and the "national delegate equivalents" each candidate had won (Bender 1983). In 1976 the Democrats established a "caucus returns headquarters" in Des Moines with a telephone reporting system from each of Iowa's ninety-nine counties, and they continue to use this statewide reporting and analysis system.

It is important to keep in mind that all Democratic caucus returns since 1972 have been projections or "delegate equivalents," not raw vote totals. The Iowa Democrats do not tabulate levels of candidate support at the caucuses after the initial division into preference groups, which would be in effect a straw poll. Rather, they count the number of people as reconstituted into viable preference groups. Using the final viable groups, they weight and then project each presidential candidate's strength at the state convention and at the national convention. (The weighting is necessary because each county sets the size of its convention, and since very small counties may hold large conventions, the weighting brings county delegate totals into proportion with their assigned delegate strength at the state convention.) This reporting system undoubtedly proves confusing to some, but the Iowa Democrats believe it provides the most accurate data available (*DMR* Oct. 16, 1983, 2C).

Republican Procedures. The Iowa Republicans' delegate selection process in presidential years is less complex. They normally elect delegates to county conventions on an at-large basis, although individual caucuses determine their own selection procedures, and, should they desire, they may elect delegates on a proportional basis. A precinct electing six delegates at large would allow each caucus participant to vote for as many as six delegates, and the individuals receiving the most votes would be elected regardless of their presidential preference (Republican Party of Iowa 1980). Conceivably, a well-organized candidate organization could pack a caucus and, with a simple majority, control all the delegates elected, a feat that would require the support of 85 percent of the participants at a Democratic caucus.

Before 1976, Republican caucuses forwarded reports to the state party headquarters in Des Moines which included the names of persons selected to attend county conventions as delegates. The caucus reports did not include the candidate preference of those elected, and it was usually several days after the caucuses before most of the reports arrived in Des Moines (Brown 1983). Since the Republican at-large system did not lend itself to projecting "delegate equivalents," changes were necessary to provide results. In 1976 the Iowa Republicans initiated a presidential preference poll and a system for reporting results to Des Moines on the evening of the caucuses. Beginning modestly, in 1976 sixty-two randomly selected precincts conducted a straw poll, but in 1980 all caucuses did so (Brown 1983). The poll is taken prior to delegate selection, and there is no requirement that the delegates elected later in the evening reflect the results of the poll. Delegates are not committed or bound to any candidate.

The 1972 Precinct Caucuses

The Iowa Democratic caucuses were scheduled for January 24, making them the nation's first
nominating event. The Iowa Republicans had not changed
their process, and they scheduled precinct caucuses for
April 4. The Iowa Democratic meetings also were the first
nominating event to use the reformed party rules that had
grown out of the McGovern-Fraser Commission. The heart
of the reforms, proportional representation, was designed
to limit the influence of the party bosses and open the entire caucus and convention system to the influence of the
grass-roots participants. Thus the Iowa Democrats, and
some national correspondents, watched closely to see if
the caucus process would be affected by the new rules and
the early date.

The Democratic Caucuses.   Senator
George McGovern appears to have been the first presidential candidate to comprehend the potential significance of
the early Iowa caucuses. Eager to dispel the conventional
wisdom that he could not win the Democratic nomination,
McGovern's national staff began putting together an organization in Iowa in the summer of 1971, several months
before the other candidates. Through the fall and winter,
local volunteers and "border-runners" from McGovern's
home state of South Dakota identified McGovern supporters and organized them in preparation for the January
caucuses (*Newsweek* Jan. 24, 1972, 15). The grass-roots,
McCarthy-style campaign stressed McGovern's lack of ties
to special interests and emphasized his desire to win the
support of the average citizen of Iowa and the nation. Although he personally campaigned in Iowa for only three
days before the caucuses, McGovern explained his major
organizational effort in a January 12, 1972, Cedar Rapids
speech. "Iowa is terribly important in the presidential
nomination," he declared. "It is the first state in the nation

where we get any test at all'' (Flansburg 1972a, 3).

Senator Edmund Muskie, although slow to organize an Iowa campaign, eventually sent full-time campaigners to supplement his local workers in hopes of demonstrating that their candidate's front-runner image was deserved (Miller 1972, 1, 25). Muskie campaign officials had built up the press's expectations about Iowa by claiming that the local caucuses in Iowa and Arizona would demonstrate early strength for their candidate (Hart 1973, 112). The Muskie campaign received a boost shortly before the precinct caucuses when the very powerful and popular Iowa senator Harold Hughes endorsed fellow senator Muskie's presidential candidacy. Hughes, who had previously refused to endorse McGovern, made a joint appearance with Muskie in Des Moines on January 18 and bestowed his blessing on him. The endorsement, which McGovern's campaign manager, Gary Hart, later called "one of the bitterest blows of the campaign" (Hart 1973, 89), was invaluable for Muskie, as it put "virtually all the key figures in the Hughes organization into the Muskie camp" (Risser 1972, 4).

Agents for other candidates made very limited efforts in Iowa in 1972. Supporters of Senator Hubert Humphrey started too late to have any real chance of doing well, and he ultimately urged his supporters to back uncommitted delegates at the precinct caucuses (Miller 1972, 25). Unable to win, Humphrey's only hope was to deny an outright victory to the other candidates, and to pursue that end he came to Iowa on January 24. There was also an unsuccessful "draft Kennedy" campaign early and a late attempt by former senator Eugene McCarthy, who had been so successful in the 1968 Iowa caucuses. In 1972, however, when McCarthy appeared in Des Moines on January 22 the old fervor was missing, and without an organization he was not a viable candidate in Iowa (O'Shea 1972, 4B).

On Monday, January 24, the night of the Democratic precinct caucuses, Iowa was under seige by a fierce winter

Iowa is well known for its harsh winters, and on several occasions the weather has had an impact on the precinct caucuses. In 1972, blizzard conditions forced the Democrats to postpone their caucuses in a number of counties. The meetings were eventually held, but in some cases they met two days after the scheduled date.

storm, and in approximately one-fourth of the state's ninety-nine counties the meetings had to be postponed until Tuesday, and in some cases Wednesday. The caucuses were conducted according to the new party rules in the remaining counties, and with a few notable exceptions (such as precinct 70 in Des Moines, where charges of rules violations surfaced), they went quite smoothly (Johnson 1972, 1).

The national news media were present in modest numbers, with approximately thirty to forty reporters on hand to observe the caucuses for the first time, lending credibility to McGovern's earlier observation about the new role Iowa would assume in the presidential nominating process (Hart 1973, 114). Included among the reporters were representatives of the national networks, the wire services, and the *Washington Post* and *New York Times* (Schier 1980, 145). The *Des Moines Register*, which is a statewide newspaper widely respected throughout the nation, played up the first-in-the-nation status of the caucuses for several days before and after the meetings.

To accommodate the media need for "hard data," state party officials made an attempt to compile statewide results on the evening of the caucuses, an effort that was complicated by the snowstorm. Using sample precincts, the officials calculated the number of delegates won by the candidates at succeeding levels in the caucus and convention process. They produced two sets of numbers. The first, the set of "national delegate equivalents," was a projection of each candidate's delegate strength at the national convention assuming that delegate loyalties did not change between the caucuses and the national convention, which is a very weak assumption.

The second set of numbers, which Democratic officials referred to as "state delegate equivalents," proved confusing to reporters unfamiliar with the complicated reporting system. The confusion is illustrated by the variety of labels used to report the Iowa results. The *New York Times* on January 26 called them delegates, and although it was not

clear, by implication this meant delegates to county conventions; the *Washington Post* that day incorrectly referred to the results as votes, and the *Des Moines Register*
on January 26 correctly termed the outcomes "state delegate equivalents" and the article explained how they had
been derived. The confusion is understandable, since the
"state delegate equivalents" were actually weighted
county delegates, and to this day few reporters understand
the complicated process by which the caucus results are
derived. (In 1984, with literally hundreds of reporters on
hand, party officials held press workshops in an attempt to
overcome the confusion about the caucus results, but they
were not very successful in clarifying the complex
process.)

The results produced by the Democratic tally were of
dubious validity, but they were nationally reported nonetheless. The results, based on partial returns of sample
precincts, are shown in Table 4.1.

Senator McGovern's organizational effort in Iowa paid
great dividends. Even though he finished third in the contest for delegates, behind "uncommitted" and Senator
Muskie, it was better than most reporters had expected,
and as we have come to learn, political reality in the electronic age is determined by the media's perception of political events. The media perception that Muskie was the
1972 Democratic front-runner and that McGovern was an
also-ran apparently was based in large part on a January

Table 4.1. 1972 Democratic Precinct Caucus Results

	State delegate equivalents (%)	Projected national delegates
Uncommitted	35.8	18
Muskie	35.5	18
McGovern	22.6	10
Humphrey	1.6	0
McCarthy	1.4	0
Chisholm	1.3	0
Jackson	1.1	0
Others	0.7	0

Source: Data from Apple 1972b, 16.

1972 Gallup poll showing that nationally 32 percent of the Democrats supported Muskie while only 3 percent favored McGovern for the party's presidential nomination (Gallup 1972, 4B). Having established who should and who should not be viewed as a serious Democratic presidential contender, the media evaluated the results of the precinct caucuses according to these expectations.

Although national coverage of the 1972 caucuses was sporadic, the media interpretation of the results cast a shadow over the Muskie campaign. The *New York Times* published stories for three consecutive days after the Iowa local meetings on January 25, 26, and 27, and in one, R. W. Apple said he thought that Muskie's victory was "clouded by the unexpected strong showing of Senator George McGovern" (1972b, 16). A *Washington Post* article stated that the results "gave no new impetus to the Muskie campaign" (Chapman 1972, A4). The stories in both the *Times* and the *Post* noted that Muskie was the winner in Iowa, and in the January 26 article Apple concluded that the Muskie victory "was big enough to insure that politicians across the country would not think that he had stumbled in Iowa." Apple observed, however, that the margin "was not big enough to add much to the bandwagon psychology he has been building" (Apple 1972b, 16). Bill Lawrence, reporting on the ABC evening news, viewed the outcome slightly differently. Much to the glee of McGovern's campaign manager, Gary Hart, he reported that "the Muskie bandwagon slid off an icy road in Iowa last night" (Hart 1973, 115).

The reporting of the 1972 Democratic precinct caucuses is consistent with the findings of later research into the media and presidential campaigns, which concludes that "candidates who do better than expected in the race do better than anybody else in attracting coverage" (Robinson and Sheehan 1983, 80). The Iowa coverage emphasized the surprisingly strong showing of McGovern and provided his campaign with access to the media.

The reporting of the 1972 Democratic caucuses was an

excellent example of Patterson's "expectations game." Senator Muskie was expected to win in Iowa, and the media had not identified a significant challenger. Senator McGovern fared much better than expected and "surprised" reporters took note of his campaign. Media interpretation of the 1972 caucus outcomes enhanced the prestige of the Iowa caucuses while providing a tremendous boost to the McGovern presidential campaign.

Projections versus Reality. A central theme of this book is that projections based on precinct caucuses are invalid and unreliable indicators of presidential candidate strength in Iowa. They are invalid because no votes are taken anywhere in the process, and delegates selected as loyal to a particular presidential candidate may not actually be supporting that candidate. Supporters of candidates who do not meet the 15 percent threshold for viability, for example, frequently align with any group willing to give them some representation on the delegation to the county convention. Thus the delegate totals for any given candidate may include supporters of other candidates as well.

The fluidity and duration of the caucus and convention system also limit the reliability of projections. The projections of delegate strength for presidential candidates are based on the assumption that campaign conditions will not change between the January 24 precinct caucuses and the state and national conventions held months later. An examination of the political events that occurred in 1972 between the January 24 caucuses and the July 9 Democratic National Convention demonstrates the projections' lack of reliability. The outcomes of ninety-eight of Iowa's ninety-nine county conventions are shown in Table 4.2. The county convention results show that both Muskie and McGovern gained strength as uncommitted delegates began to commit to one of the candidates. Although it does happen that large numbers of delegates remain uncommit-

Table 4.2.   1972 Democratic County Convention Results

	State delegates (%)	Projected national delegates
Muskie	39.3	19
Uncommitted	30.7	14
McGovern	28.2	13
Others	2.2	0

Source: Data from Flansburg 1972b, 1, 8.

ted all the way to the national convention, it is not uncommon for their number to dwindle as the campaign progresses.

On March 25 the district conventions, which were held separately from the state meeting for the first time as a result of the new Iowa rules, elected thirty-four of the forty-six delegates to the national convention, with the following loyalties: Muskie 14, McGovern 12, and uncommitted 8. Again, the winnowing process of uncommitted delegates continued, and when on April 27, after several primary election reversals, Muskie announced that he was suspending his campaign for the presidency, the race for the Democratic nomination took a new turn in Iowa with the state convention still almost a month away. One Muskie delegate immediately gave his support to McGovern, a few began to look around for another candidate, and the remaining thirteen Muskie delegates decided to stay the course (Flansburg 1972c, 1, 6).

By the time of the Democratic state convention in 1972 there were significant changes in the presidential campaign. The Muskie campaign was in limbo, and McGovern had emerged as a viable and strong candidate for the nomination. Yet the results reported by the media after the January 24 caucuses included projections of state delegates, numbers that were meaningless by the time of the event for which they were projected.

The state convention selected the remaining ten delegates to the national convention (the two national committee members are unelected delegates and they favored

Muskie). The results were: McGovern 5, Muskie 3, and un-committed 2. Table 4.3 is a comparison of the "national delegate equivalents" projected after the precinct caucuses in January with the expressed candidate prefer-ence of national delegates selected at the district and state conventions. The actual national delegate totals demon-strate the lack of reliability of the caucus projections. Whereas the caucus projections had McGovern in third place, he and Muskie were in a dead heat after the state convention. Moreover, the Muskie support was "soft" since he was no longer an active candidate for the presidency.

Table 4.3. 1972 Democratic National Delegate Equivalents Com-pared to National Convention Delegates

	January projection	National delegate preferences
Muskie	18	18
McGovern	10	18
Uncommitted	18	10

Source: National delegate preferences from Flansburg 1972d, 1B.

It is interesting to speculate about how the caucus re-sults might have been reported had the projections more accurately reflected the candidate leanings of the Iowa del-egation to the Democratic National Convention. The headlines of the stories in the *Times*, the *Post*, and the *Register* probably would have suggested that McGovern was a surprise big winner and that although in a virtual dead heat, the Muskie campaign had suffered a devastat-ing setback in Iowa. R. W. Apple's conclusion in the *Times* that politicians would not think that Muskie had stumbled might have been replaced by a headline stating, "Political Pros Think Muskie Stumbles Badly in Iowa." New Hampshire would have become even more important to the "faltering" Muskie campaign, and the momentum would have been with McGovern, who might have done even better in New Hampshire as the "big winner" in Iowa.

Would Muskie have been knocked out of the race earlier, and if so, would the party pros have been able to convince Hubert Humphrey, or some other mainline Democrat, to make a serious bid for the nomination? Could McGovern have survived an early front-runner status? McGovern might have prevailed anyway, but it is also possible that the reporting of the Iowa media event and its inaccurate projections altered the outcome of the 1972 Democratic nomination.

A final comment about the 1972 Democratic caucuses concerns the implementation of party reforms. The proportional representation procedure was carefully followed at all levels of the caucus and convention system in Iowa, and whereas the state's 1968 national delegates had been appointed (following tradition) by Governor Harold Hughes, the 1972 national delegates were elected, and they included many from the rank and file. Although the party's affirmative action goal was not completely met, over 40 percent of the delegation were women, and other traditionally underrepresented groups were included as well. The only apparent negative side effect of the revised rules was the increased length of the party sessions at every level caused by the proportional representation requirement (Flansburg and O'Shea 1972, 1, 10).

The Republican Caucuses. In 1972 the Iowa Republicans did not hold their caucuses until April 4, and thus they missed out on the national attention attracted by the Democrats. President Richard Nixon was not actively opposed in Iowa, although Ohio congressman John Ashbrook, who was challenging the president in some states, did receive a few votes in straw polls. There was little controversy, and the meetings received very limited space even in the local press (Johnson and Hansen 1972, 1). The Republican caucuses, whose procedures were unchanged from 1968, received no national attention.

The Iowa precinct caucuses emerged as a weather vane for political experts after the 1972 presidential race. The *New York Times* and *Washington Post* were among the few national media who covered the 1972 Iowa caucuses. But, after missing the signs of weakness in the 1972 Muskie campaign, the national media converged on Iowa in 1976 to gather information about the progress of the presidential nominating races.

64

The Impact of the
1972 Caucuses

The Iowa caucuses alerted the nation that the presidential candidacy of Senator Edmund Muskie was vulnerable. Although the media coverage was modest, significant attention by the news trendsetters—the *New York Times* and the *Washington Post*—and the postcaucus success of the McGovern campaign assured more extensive media attention and a larger role for the Iowa caucuses in succeeding years.

Of greater importance, the 1972 caucuses marked the beginning of a dramatic change in American electoral politics. As the impact of the Iowa caucuses continued to grow in succeeding years, other states would move their primary elections and caucuses to earlier in the presidential nominating season. The traditional four-month primary season beginning in New Hampshire in March and culminating in California in June would be significantly altered. The schedule of primary events would be compressed and a new front-loaded season emphasizing the nominating processes in Iowa, New Hampshire, and South Dakota would develop. The traditionally late primary in California would be of little importance in future years, because presidential nominating races would be decided by the earlier events.

References

Apple, R. W., Jr. 1972a. "Iowa Democrats Hold Caucuses, First Step in Picking Delegates." *New York Times*, January 25, p. 20L.

_____. 1972b. "Muskie Is Victor in Iowa Caucuses." *New York Times*, January 26, p. 16.

_____. 1972c. "Heavy Turnout by Iowa Students Said to Have Had Role in Outcome of Democratic Precinct Caucuses." *New York Times*, January 27, p. 19.

Bender, Richard. 1983. Telephone interview with author, March 23. Bender was the director of operations of the Iowa Democratic party from 1970 to 1975.

Brown, Ralph. 1983. Telephone interview with author, March 16. Brown was the executive director of the Iowa Republican party from 1975 to 1977.

Chapman, William. 1972. "Iowa Caucuses Back Muskie, 33% Undecided." *Washington Post*, January 26, p. A4.

Clifton, C. C. 1952. "Huge Turnout by Republican Voters in D.M." *Des Moines Register*, March 8, p. 1.

Crotty, William, and John S. Jackson III. 1985. *Presidential Primaries and Nominations*. Washington, D.C.: CQ Press.

Des Moines Register. 1952–83.

Flansburg, James. 1972a. "Iowa Swing by McGovern in Demo Bid." *Des Moines Register*, January 13, pp. 1, 3.

_____. 1972b. "Democrats Hold County Parleys." *Des Moines Register*, February 28, pp. 1, 8.

_____. 1972c. "State Democratic Leader Sees Muskie Out of Race." *Des Moines Register*, April 28, pp. 1, 6.

_____. 1972d. "McGovern and Muskie Split." *Des Moines Register*, May 21, p. 1B.

Flansburg, James, and James O'Shea. 1972. "McGovern Gains Strength in 20-Hour State Parley." *Des Moines Register*, May 22, pp. 1, 10.

Gallup, George. 1972. "Muskie Leads Kennedy in Survey of Democrats." *Des Moines Register*, January 23, p. 4B.

Hart, Gary. 1973. *Right from the Start: A Chronicle of the McGovern Campaign*. New York: Quadrangle Books.

Iowa Democratic Party. 1980. Precinct Caucus Kit, 1980. Mimeographed.

_____. 1984a. Constitution. Amended 1984.

_____. 1984b. Precinct Caucus Kit. Mimeographed.

Johnson, Stephen M. 1972. "See Caucus 'Packed' in Precinct 70." *Des Moines Register*, January 27, pp. 1, 7.

Johnson, Stephen M., and Christine Hansen. 1972. "Report Little Controversy at Republican Caucuses." *Des Moines Register*, April 5, pp. 1, 7.

Larson, Clifton. 1981. Telephone interview with author, February 23. Larson was the chair of the Iowa Democratic party from 1970 to 1973.

_____. 1983. Telephone interview with author, March 27.

Miller, Norman. 1972. "As Iowa Goes . . . ?" *Wall Street Journal*, January 19, pp. 1, 25.

Mills, George. 1968a. "Iowa G.O.P. in Caucuses." *Des Moines Register*, March 4, p. 9.

_____. 1968b. "Add Fire to Already Hot Party Battle." *Des Moines Register*, March 17, pp. 1, 3.

_____. 1968c. "Foes Capture Large Share of Delegates." *Des Moines Register*, March 27, pp. 1, 3.

_____. 1968d. "Rasmussen Tells of 'Irregularities.' " *Des Moines Register*, April 4, pp. 1, 3.

Newsweek. 1972.

O'Shea, James. 1972. "McCarthy Fans' Fervor Missing." *Des Moines Register*, January 23, p. 4B.

Patterson, Thomas E. 1980. *The Mass Media Election: How Americans Choose Their President*. New York: Praeger.

Republican Party of Iowa. 1980. Suggested Procedure for Precinct Caucuses, January 21, 1980. Mimeographed.

_____. 1983. Conducting Your Precinct Caucus. Mimeographed.

_____. 1984. Constitution. Amended 1984.

Risser, James. 1972. "Muskie Wins Support of Senator Hughes." *Des Moines Register*, January 18, pp. 1, 4.

Robinson, Michael J., and Margaret A. Sheehan. 1983. *Over the Wire and on TV: CBS and UPI in Campaign '80*. New York: Russell Sage Foundation.

Schier, Steven E. 1980. *The Rules of the Game: Democratic National Convention Delegate Selection in Iowa and Wisconsin*. Washington, D.C.: University Press of America.

Seplow, Stephen. 1968. "Hughes Says Johnson 'No' Shocks Him." *Des Moines Register*, April 1, pp. 1, 10.

Weaver, Warren. 1968. "McCarthy Gets About 40%, Johnson and Nixon on Top in New Hampshire Voting." *New York Times*, March 13, pp. 1, 33.

★★★★★ 5 ★★★★★★★★★

The 1976 Caucuses:
The Making of a
Front-Runner

The national news media, with notable exceptions, devoted minimal time and space to the 1972 Iowa precinct caucuses. The limited coverage is understandable, given the newness of Iowa as an early source of information about the progress of the presidential campaign, but it also is apparent that the media fell victim to their own expectations about the 1972 presidential nominations. Reporters made up their minds early in 1972 about the likely outcome of the presidential nominating contests. President Nixon would certainly be renominated by the Republicans, and according to Donald R. Mathews, "political pundits nearly to a man had predicted that Senator Ed Muskie of Maine would be the Democratic nominee" (1978, 58).

Thus the Iowa caucuses remained relatively anonymous. Senator McGovern's grass-roots effort went largely unnoticed, receiving minimal coverage by the major newspapers and television networks, whose focus, Jules Witcover has said, "was squarely on Muskie as he collected big-name endorsements en route, nearly everyone thought, to a routine first-ballot nomination" (1977, 200). When Muskie's 1972 presidential campaign collapsed in late April, political reporters found themselves in a very embarrassing position: The man they had already "nominated" was no longer a candidate for the presidency. News reporters badly underestimated the potential of McGovern's grass-roots organizational effort and had failed to discover the signs of weakness in the Muskie campaign. Additionally, although the Watergate break-in took place during the campaign, it went undetected when President Nixon escaped the careful eye of the press by conducting a rose-garden campaign. The 1972 mistakes were harmful to the credibility of the reporters who covered presidential nominations, and thus, said Witcover, "in 1976, if there were going to be early signals, the fourth estate was going to be on the scene en masse to catch them" (1977, 200).

Precaucus Activity

Meanwhile, the Iowa parties were taking steps to expand the nation's interest in their caucuses. The Iowa Republicans, who missed out on the headlines in 1972 by holding their meetings in April, were anxious to share the limelight with the Democrats. Both parties realized the desirability for media purposes of a common date. They arranged a marriage of convenience to hold the 1976 caucuses on January 19, and they have continued the practice in presidential years. As previously discussed, the Republicans initiated a straw poll in selected precincts, and the Democrats developed a statewide system for reporting delegate totals in 1976. Thus the stage was set for a truly national media event, and Iowa's party leaders were not to be disappointed.

The Democratic Campaign. Jimmy Carter targeted Iowa as a testing ground for his campaign and spent nearly a year cultivating a following. Virtually unknown outside the South, Carter endured some very difficult days in the effort to put together a grass-roots organization in Iowa. In reminiscing about his first visit to Des

Jimmy Carter, commonly referred to as "Jimmy Who" in the early stages of the 1976 race for the presidency, used the Iowa caucuses as a springboard to the Democratic nomination. In his early visits to Iowa he spoke to small crowds in obscure places, but his patience and systematic approach to organizing the state paid great dividends when the media interpreted the results of the 1976 meetings as a great victory for Carter.

Moines in February 1975, Carter recalled a reception held at a local hotel: "There were Jody and myself and the man and woman who arranged the reception—and I think there were three other people" (Schram 1977, 6). Overcoming the embarrassment, Democratic state chair Tom Whitney suggested to Jody Powell that he be given a few minutes to make arrangements for a Carter visit to the courthouse, where he at least shook a few hands and met some Polk County Democrats (Whitney 1986).

The day before, on February 26, Carter had been the featured speaker at a dinner in Le Mars honoring Marie Jahn, who was retiring after thirty-eight years as the Plymouth County recorder (Flansburg 1975a, 34). Perhaps the testimonial dinner was not significant enough to attract a presidential candidate, but Carter was not flooded with invitations in those early Iowa days. After the Le Mars speech Carter campaigned two more days in Iowa, and the extended visit proved well worth the effort. He received extensive coverage in the *Des Moines Register*—four days of stories—and impressed chief political writer James Flansburg. In a front-page article Flansburg praised Carter's knowledge of the issues and observed that "seldom has a candidate without a fabled name made such a fast and favorable impression on Iowans" (1975b, 1).

Carter, who had earlier decided to make a major effort in New Hampshire and Florida, concluded that he could do well in Iowa, and furthermore, he perceived that he had the opportunity to turn the precinct caucuses into a major media event (Schram 1977, 6). In those early days, the Carter campaign did not have a great deal of competition in Iowa, because, according to Witcover, "other candidates and prospective candidates concentrated most of their pre-election year energies in minor liberal skirmishes in the East or on New Hampshire" (1977, 197). By late August 1975 campaign aide Tim Kraft had persuaded those directing the national effort that he should move full-time into Iowa, and he set out to organize the state. Rather than appoint an Iowa campaign chair and risk being saddled with that person's political image, he put together a group (nineteen or twenty people depending on whom you read) called the "Iowa Carter for President Steering Committee," which was geographically and ideologically representative and which included some very important Democrats (Schram 1977, 9).

In less than a month, the Kraft effort yielded concrete results in the September 22 "off-year caucuses" held throughout the state. The enterprising Whitney was committed to making the Iowa caucuses a media event, and he had decided that a straw poll might enliven the meetings and draw some media attention. Some 5762 people participated in the poll, and although the results were inconclusive, Carter came in first. He received 9.9 percent of the vote, Sargent Shriver received 8.7 percent, Birch Bayh 8.1, Hubert Humphrey 7.2, Henry Jackson 6.5, Morris Udall 6.1, and Fred Harris 5.7. A total of 45 percent of the participants were uncommitted, and the remaining 3 percent of the votes were broadly scattered. (*DMR* Oct. 25, 1975, 1). The results may have shed little light on the Democratic race, but the poll served to notify reporters that Iowa would provide "an early line on the 1976 contenders," and they were paying close attention when the next poll was held at the Jefferson-Jackson Day dinner in Ames on October 25 (Witcover 1977, 201).

By late October 1975 the field of candidates for the Democratic presidential nomination had grown substantially. In addition to those noted above, Terry Sanford, Lloyd Bentsen, and Milton Shapp were announced candidates, and George Wallace was considered a strong contender for the nomination. These latter four candidates, however, spent little or no time campaigning in Iowa. In fact, prior to the Jefferson-Jackson Day dinner only Carter, Harris, Shriver, Jackson, and Udall had made major efforts in the state, and the quality of their campaigns was mixed.

Senator Henry Jackson began his caucus effort as early as Carter, but he gained little visibility even though he campaigned frequently in Iowa. By mid-1975 he had withdrawn from the state. Former senator Fred Harris started in Iowa nearly as early as Carter and spent an immense amount of time and effort courting delegates, but he was plagued by limited funds and uneven organization. Sargent Shriver, the 1972 vice-presidential nominee, was also an early starter in Iowa and had hoped to appeal to the heavily Catholic areas of the state, but despite frequent visits, he was unable to persuade local Democratic leaders that his campaign should be taken seriously (Schier 1980, 295–308).

Representative Morris Udall established a presence in Iowa early in 1975, but he targeted few resources for the precinct caucuses. His campaign staff was instead focusing on the New Hampshire primary, which traditionally attracts great media attention as the nation's first primary election. They hoped that success in New Hampshire would be followed by victories in Massachusetts and Wisconsin (Arterton 1978a, 15–17). Senator Birch Bayh announced for the presidency just a few days before the Jefferson-Jackson Day dinner.

This dinner is an important event for Iowa Democrats. It is the major fund-raiser of the year, and it brings large numbers of the faithful together for a huge pep rally. In recent presidential years it has also provided an opportunity to showcase the Iowa Democratic party. Held in the fall, it is timed perfectly for Democratic presidential candidates to appear and make their case before the partisans most likely to attend the precinct caucuses a few months later. In 1976, for the first time, a large number of the presidential hopefuls attended and spoke at the dinner in Ames.

The Ames gathering, choreographed by State Chair Whitney, was political theater at its best. All the presidential candidates were invited, and the affair, according to Jules Witcover, "had all the trappings of a political convention, with booths set up at the back of the arena for each of the hopefuls, and time set aside . . . to man the booths, shake hands, and answer questions" (1977, 201). George

McGovern, the 1972 Democratic standard-bearer, was the keynote speaker. Seven presidential candidates attended—Bayh, Carter, Harris, Jackson, Sanford, Shriver, and Udall—and they were permitted ten minutes each for speeches, followed by demonstrations of support. All the candidates held beer-and-wine receptions after the dinner activities (Flansburg 1975d, 1A; Flansburg 1975e, 1A, 14A).

The *Des Moines Register*, however, was the key actor at the Jefferson-Jackson Day dinner. The paper, using its own polling organization, arranged a straw poll that Flansburg said "was conducted before the candidates spoke, in an effort to measure organizational effectiveness" (1975f, 1A). Ballots were distributed to the fifty-dollar-a-couple, full-paying guests, but balcony seats were available for two dollars (minus the meal), and Tim Kraft had packed the balcony with Carter supporters, some of whom managed to vote in the poll (Witcover 1977, 201). The results of the poll are shown in Table 5.1.

Carter was judged the big winner in the Jefferson-Jackson Day poll. The *Register* story ran under the headline "Carter Tops Democratic Straw Poll," with the

Table 5.1.   1975 Jefferson-Jackson Day Poll Results

	Votes	Percentage of total votes
Carter	256	23.4
Humphrey	135	12.3
Bayh	112	10.2
Shriver	93	8.5
Udall	77	7.0
Harris	61	5.6
Jackson	56	5.1
Sanford	7	0.6
Wallace	6	0.5
Bentsen	2	0.2
Shapp	2	0.2
Write-ins	47	4.3
Undecided	240	21.9
	1094	99.8

Source: Data from Flansburg 1975f, 1A.

added subtitle, "Other Contenders Trail Far Behind" (Flansburg 1975f, 1A). The *New York Times*, in a story headline of perhaps record length, declared: "Carter Appears to Hold a Solid Lead in Iowa as the Campaign's First Test Approaches." In the *Times* article R. W. Apple noted that Carter "has made dramatic progress while attention was focused on the scramble for liberal primacy among Mr. Udall, Mr. Bayh, Mr. Harris, and Mr. Shriver." Apple concluded that Carter "appears to have taken a surprising but solid lead for Iowa's 47 delegates to the Democratic National Convention next year" (Oct. 27, 1975, 17L).

The Apple article provided a tremendous boost for Carter because it focused national media attention on his campaign. According to Elizabeth Drew, the Apple story "was itself a political event, prompting other newspaper stories that Carter was doing well in Iowa, and then more newsmagazine and television coverage for Carter than might otherwise have been his share" (Arterton 1978b, 39). Reporters from *Time* and *Newsweek* indicated that their magazines had decided to pay greater attention to the Iowa caucuses as a result of the Apple story and one by Jules Witcover in the *Washington Post* (Arterton 1978b, 39). Others have noted that "the *Times* and, to a lesser degree, the *Post* are the media's references for subjects to be covered" (Paletz and Entman 1981, 7), and that seems to have been the case with the Iowa caucuses. The two papers were among the few that had covered the 1972 caucuses extensively, and now they pointed the way in 1976.

After eight months of hard work at the grass-roots level, a victory in the Jefferson-Jackson Day straw poll, and a story in the *New York Times*, Carter was now the front-runner in Iowa. He had been judged a viable candidate by the news media on the basis of very soft evidence: his apparent organizational skills and his straw-poll successes. Now, however, a new set of expectations had been created. As the front-runner, Carter would have to win, or at least do very well, in the Iowa caucuses. A campaign worker observed that "if we don't finish first or a close

The 1976 campaign in Iowa was characterized by straw polls. Democratic leaders discovered that they could increase interest in and attract media attention to a gathering or fund-raiser by holding a well-publicized straw poll. The results of a poll conducted by the *Des Moines Register* at the Jefferson-Jackson Day dinner in 1975 were reported nationally and made Carter the front-runner in Iowa.

second, . . . I'm afraid the press will crucify us. I think I liked it better when we were underdogs" (Hunt 1976, 20).

Udall, who after the campaign referred to the *Register* survey as "that silly poll in Iowa" (Schram 1977, 16), recognized the new reality and altered his strategy to include more time and money for Iowa. He committed ten days in January and approximately $80,000 of his limited campaign funds to the state. An aide justified the investment by the potential for media exposure, observing that the caucuses "will be covered like the first primary always has been in the national press," and he reasoned that "Iowa justifies the expense" (Witcover 1977, 204).

Senator Bayh, who had done surprisingly well in the Jefferson-Jackson Day poll in spite of his late start, also decided to make a major effort to gain support in the precinct caucuses. He was not alone. As the January caucuses approached, presidential hopefuls were so common in Iowa that a State Center couple reported seeing all the Democratic candidates at least twice without ever having driven "more than an hour from their home" (Flansburg 1976a, 16A). With the emphasis on organization and personal contact at the grass-roots level, five of the 1976 Democratic candidates spent more time in Iowa than the combined seven campaign days of the 1972 candidates. Table 5.2 shows the number of campaign days that the most active candidates spent in Iowa. There were also infrequent visits by other candidates, such as Terry Sanford's appearance at the Jefferson-Jackson Day dinner.

Table 5.2. 1976 Democratic Precaucus Campaign Activity

	Days in Iowa
Harris	23
Carter	17
Bayh	15
Shriver	13
Udall	12
Jackson	6

Source: Data from Flansburg 1976c, 7A.

A final political event that contributed to media expectations about the upcoming Iowa caucuses occurred one week before the January 19 date of the meetings. The *New York Times* ran a front-page story by R. W. Apple rating the presidential chances of the 1976 Democratic candidates. On the basis of his conversations with political pros in a number of early caucus and primary states, Apple divided the hopefuls into three groups: (1) those "most likely to be selected"—Jackson, Bayh, Carter, and Humphrey; (2) those with "a conceivable chance of being nominated"— Shriver, Harris, and Udall; and finally (3) "those most unlikely to be the nominee"—Bentsen, Shapp, Sanford, Church, Wallace, and Byrd. Apple conceded that "such early calculations are highly speculative" but asserted that media perception of the nominating campaign becomes the all-important reality against which caucus and primary outcomes are judged (Apple 1976a, 1, 19). Political reporters had developed their expectations about the Democratic race for the presidential nomination, and now they awaited the "hard news" that the first caucuses and primaries would provide.

The Republican Campaign. Normally it is the caucuses of the "out party" that provide the excitement, but in 1976 interest in the Republican caucuses increased when Governor Ronald Reagan decided to challenge President Gerald Ford for the nomination. Precaucus media coverage of the Republican meetings was very limited, however, compared to that given the Democrats. Writing about the Republican caucuses shortly before their scheduled date, one reporter explained the disparity this way: "Neither President Ford nor his challenger, Ronald Reagan, has chosen to pay much attention to the Republican caucuses, . . . so the press hasn't either" (Hunt 1976, 1). Supporters of the two candidates made some effort to organize in Iowa, but it was a low-visibility campaign.

There was a certain novelty in a challenge to a sitting

president, but Reagan had made no secret of his presidential aspirations. Moreover, Ford was perceived as vulnerable. He had been appointed vice-president by President Nixon when Spiro Agnew resigned under a cloud of scandal, and he succeeded to the presidency when Mr. Nixon resigned as a result of Watergate. Ford had not been elected to either office, and when he pardoned the former president for all Watergate crimes, the conventional wisdom held that Ford's reelection was in jeopardy. Those who reported and those who followed politics were anxious for hard news to confirm or disprove Ford's vulnerability. But President Ford chose not to campaign in Iowa.

Reagan did make a brief appearance in Iowa on the Saturday before the caucuses, when the plane taking him from New Hampshire to California landed in Des Moines to refuel and give the candidate an opportunity to hold an airport rally. About 300 people attended and questioned Reagan about his stands on current political issues, including his proposal to shift many social programs from federal to state jurisdiction (Flansburg 1976b, 5A).

The 1976 Precinct Caucuses

The precinct caucuses operated under a new law passed by the general assembly in 1975. Concerned that participation and democratic processes suffered in overcrowded private homes, the legislature required that precinct caucuses be held in public buildings wherever possible (Ia. Gen. Assem. 1975, chap. 81, p. 162). Since that time, more caucuses have been held in public buildings, but many rural and small-town meetings are still held in private homes.

The Democratic Caucuses.　On caucus night the Democrats established a "caucus returns head-

quarters" at the Des Moines Hilton, with a telephone reporting system from each of Iowa's ninety-nine counties.
Party staff were available for analysis, and they provided
state delegate equivalents and national delegate equivalents from the precinct caucuses. State Chair Tom Whitney, who was rapidly becoming the P. T. Barnum of electoral politics, organized a media-watching event in the
grand ballroom of the Hilton. He reasoned that with so
many national media dignitaries in attendance, there was
money to be made, and he sold tickets to anyone willing to
pay ten dollars for the opportunity to watch the reporters
in action. Drinks were sold for a dollar, and everyone had a
good time watching media stars like Roger Mudd and Herbert Kaplow work (Hollobaugh 1976, 7A). Whitney discovered, however, that it was not always easy to deal with the
big egos of the press. The *Los Angeles Times* staff, for example, upon discovering that their seats were in the second row, complained that they should be in the front row
with the *New York Times* and the *Washington Post*. The
media-watching event made about $4,000 for the party
(Whitney 1986).

News reporters contributed to the growth of the Iowa
media event by extensively covering the 1976 caucus results as the first hard news in the presidential contest.
Most of the major national print and broadcast media sent
representatives to cover the process, and the three
networks planned live caucus coverage on January 19
(Schier 1980, 316). The networks did not, however, set up
temporary studios or move their news anchors to Des
Moines, as they would for future presidential caucuses.
Party officials estimated that 150 reporters were on hand
the day of the caucuses and that each of the three
networks had another three dozen people in the state to
cover the event (Hunt 1976, 1, 20). "Meet the Press," with
four Democratic presidential candidates as guests, originated from Des Moines the week before the caucuses.

The day after the caucuses, the media began interpret-
ing the Iowa results to the nation. The Democratic results

are given in Table 5.3. The *New York Times* declared that Carter had "scored an impressive victory in yesterday's Iowa Democratic precinct caucuses" (Apple 1976b, 1). A *Times* story a day later began this way: "Former Gov. Jimmy Carter of Georgia found himself widely regarded today as a major contender for the Democratic nomination." Analyzing the order of finish, R. W. Apple concluded that Bayh "finished a much weaker second than he had expected" and that Udall's poor standing "raised serious questions about his staff's ability to run a national campaign." But perhaps the most novel aspect of the story was the grading of each candidate's performance in the Iowa caucuses: Carter received an A, Harris a B, Bayh a C, Udall and Shriver Ds, and Jackson an incomplete (Apple 1976c, 1, 28). The *Wall Street Journal* saw Carter as an impressive winner because of his "convincing two-to-one margin over his nearest rival," while Udall, who "ran a poor fourth in a state where he invested much effort," and Shriver, who "ran a barely visible fifth," were the big losers (Jan. 21, 1976, 8). Jules Witcover, writing in the *Washington Post*, was more cautious, noting that "Jimmy Carter has gained early momentum in the winnowing out process" although "his victory is far from decisive." Witcover went on to say that "if there were losers," they were Udall and Shriver (1976, A1, A4).

The February 2 editions of *Time*, *Newsweek*, and *U.S.*

Table 5.3.   1976 Democratic Precinct Caucus Results

	State delegate equivalents (%)	Projected national delegates
Uncommitted	37.15	18
Carter	27.63	13
Bayh	13.16	6
Harris	9.93	5
Udall	5.97	3
Shriver	3.30	2
Jackson	1.10	0
Others	1.76	0

Source: Data from unofficial results provided by the Iowa Democratic party, based on 2220 of the 2530 precincts (88%).

News and World Report included major stories about the caucuses. Most of the stories' space in the three magazines was devoted to Carter, and they characterized him as the winner or front-runner, or both. *Time* and *Newsweek*, for example, gave Carter a total of 726 lines of coverage, while Udall, Harris, Bayh, Jackson, and Shriver averaged only thirty lines each (Paletz and Entman 1981, 35). The magazines gave very little space to the other Democrats in any of the articles, although the *Time* story concluded that the Iowa caucuses were "a near disaster for Udall" (Feb. 2, 1976, 17).

Carter had spent January 19 in New York, hoping to turn an anticipated win in Iowa into a media bonanza by being available to the network morning news shows. The networks were indeed interested in Carter, and on the twentieth he appeared on NBC's "Today" show, CBS's "Morning News," and ABC's "AM America" (Schram 1977, 18). The CBS "Morning News" declared Carter the victor and conducted a rather lengthy interview with him in which he interpreted the impact of the caucuses on his and the other candidates' campaigns. The only other candidate shown during the program was Fred Harris, and he was represented as finishing a poor third (Schier 1980, 336). Carter enjoyed five times as much postcaucus television coverage as any other candidate (Paletz and Entman 1981, 35).

Media reporting of the results of the 1976 Iowa Democratic precinct caucuses was uniform: Carter was the big winner. He met all the expectations of the reporters and captured most of the news space and airtime. Carter was clearly the media front-runner going into the New Hampshire primary election. Many thought that the Bayh and Shriver campaigns had been damaged by their relatively poor showing, but virtually all the media covering the caucuses thought that Iowa had severely hurt Udall. R. W. Apple had even suggested that his campaign was of minor-league quality.

Yet Carter, the media victor, won only 28 percent of the

state delegate equivalents, and the largest category of delegates (37 percent) was the uncommitted group. Further, there would be many changes in support patterns in Iowa between the precinct caucuses and the state convention. Attributing so much importance to the Iowa caucuses is a little like establishing the opening-day winners in the major leagues as the heavy favorites to win the World Series. The difference, of course, is that the media have little impact on the outcome of the baseball season. Furthermore, participation in the caucuses was low in 1976. Party officials estimated that 4 percent (22,000 to 26,000) of the registered Republicans (Roth 1984) and 7 percent (38,500) of the eligible Democrats attended caucuses (Steffen 1984). (Caucus attendance figures are very rough estimates by party officials and must be treated carefully. In 1976, for example, Tom Whitney told reporters that 50,000 people had participated in the Democratic caucuses, and that figure was widely reported. Whitney indicated to me that he pulled that figure "off the top of his head" in response to a reporter's question about attendance. The later estimate of 38,500 by party officials is also only an estimate [Steffen 1984].) It is little wonder that Michael J. Robinson classified "Carter's media victory in Iowa" as one of the major "medialities" of the 1976 presidential election (1981, 196).

The Validity of the Democratic Results. Less than a week after the precinct caucuses, the staff of the *Des Moines Register* discovered a problem with the 1976 Democratic results. The numbers released to the media by the Iowa Democrats were misleading because the party had not followed its own 15 percent rule in calculating state and national delegates. As indicated in Table 5.3, party officials projected thirteen national delegates for Carter and a total of sixteen for four other candidates—Bayh, Harris, Udall, and Shriver. In analyzing the figures provided by Democratic headquarters, the *Register* found that "Carter was the only candidate to win enough support to guarantee him some Iowa delegates" and that "none of the other candidates [was] close to having enough support to win one single delegate." Although the 15 percent rule was followed in selecting county delegates, State Chair Whitney readily conceded that in calculating the state delegate equivalents and projecting beyond the county party officials ignored the binding rule and instead used a 5 percent threshold. Whitney said this was done so that the "results would be clear-cut and show the rank-and-file sentiment for each of the candidates" (Flansburg 1976d, 1A, 5A). Table 5.4 shows the results of the 1976 Democratic caucuses derived by the *Register* using the 15 percent threshold required by party rules.

Table 5.4. 1976 Democratic Precinct Caucus Results, Observing the 15 Percent Rule

	State delegate equivalents		Projected national delegates
	Number	Percentage of total	
Uncommitted	1070	31.2	39
Carter	940	27.4	8
Bayh	257	7.5	0
Harris	173	5.0	0
Udall	88	2.6	0
Shriver	32	0.9	0
	2560	74.6	47

Source: Data from the *Des Moines Register* Jan. 25, 1976, 1A, 5A. The results from 2169 of 2530 precincts (86%) were obtained from the Iowa Democratic party. The absence of 14 percent of the precincts made it impossible to project the other 872 state delegates (25.4%).

The *Register* did not allege that the Iowa Democrats had violated the national Democratic party's 15 percent rule in selecting county delegates. The party did, however, mislead reporters and the nation by ignoring the rule in calculating state and national delegates. Simply stated, the results reported to the media were phony. They did not accurately reflect the delegate selection process that took place on January 19. Official Democratic results completed after all precincts had been tabulated, which were published in the Democrats' 1980 Precinct Caucus Kit, confirm the *Register*'s analysis (p. 2). It is interesting that while Iowa has many laws governing the conduct of precinct caucuses, including laws governing when and where they may be held, and making the manipulation of the outcome of a primary election illegal, no law prohibits the creation and publication of misleading caucus results.

It is very likely that media interpretations of the 1976 Democratic caucuses would have been different had they been given the results shown in Table 5.4 instead of those in Table 5.3. Carter's victory might have been seen as even more stunning, and reporters likely would have held a mass crucifixion for the also-rans who fared so poorly. R. W. Apple's report card might have been revised to something like this: Carter, A +; Bayh, D; Harris, D −; Udall and Shriver, F; and Jackson, incomplete. Or, and perhaps more likely, the story headline might have read "Iowa Uncommitted," and neither Carter nor Whitney wanted that interpretation.

It is tempting to go on in this vein, but to do so risks obscuring a major point of this book: that the Iowa precinct caucuses do not produce meaningful results. Because they represent merely the first in a multistage process, there are no reportable outcomes, and no one considered that a problem before 1972. The parties contrived results so that Iowa could become a media event; in 1976 the results were simply more contrived and deceptive than usual.

The 1976 meetings provide a good example of the problems associated with caucus projections. The mediareported Democratic projection of national delegate equivalents indicated that Carter would control 13 of Iowa's 47 national delegates, Morris Udall 3, other candidates 13, and 18 were uncommitted. As the winnowing process continued during the caucus and primary season, delegate loyalties changed—in some cases several times.

The liberal candidates dropped out one by one, and in Iowa their supporters coalesced around Morris Udall. His strength grew steadily, and after the national delegates were elected at the district and state conventions, the candidate totals looked like this: Carter 20, Udall 12, and Harris 2, with 13 uncommitted. On the first and only ballot at the Democratic National Convention in New York City, Iowa gave 25 of its 47 votes to Carter, 20 to Udall, and 1 each to Senator Ted Kennedy and Governor Jerry Brown. The disparity illustrates the danger of projecting outcomes on the basis of the first stage in a multistage process. The media did not report raw vote totals; there were none. They reported phony projections that were never accurate and by the time of the national convention were irrelevant. By that time, however, the caucuses were long forgotten, and there was no demand for accountability for the misleading "results" reported about Iowa.

The Republican Caucuses.   The Republicans hoped to stimulate citizen participation and post-caucus media coverage with their new straw poll at some of the meetings. The poll was scheduled for sixty-two randomly selected precincts picked after consulting a survey firm from Shenandoah to insure that their methods conformed with standard survey procedures. The precincts chosen for the straw poll were not revealed until the time of the caucuses to prevent packing by supporters of either Governor Reagan or President Ford (*DMR* Jan. 12, 1976, 6A). The goal of the survey was to gain knowledge about the sentiments of those attending Republican caucuses, not to predict delegate totals to county conventions, so there was no weighting of the totals (Brown 1986). Most important, the poll would provide some numbers for the media.

Media coverage of the 1976 Republican caucuses was extensive, but postcaucus stories devoted considerably less space to the Ford-Reagan contest than they did to the

Carter victory. The *New York Times* story of January 20, for example, devoted 26 lines to the Republican caucuses and 123 to the Democratic caucuses; the remaining 56 lines explained caucus procedures. The January 21 *Times* article gave 26 lines to the Republican and 357 to the Democratic caucuses. The *Times* noted that President Ford had the backing of virtually all Republican party officials but still "barely defeated" Governor Reagan in the straw poll by a vote of 264 to 248 (Apple 1976b, 1). The *Wall Street Journal* said that the straw poll gave Ford a "narrow lead" over Reagan, but it more or less dismissed the poll because it was not an "indicator of how Iowa's delegation will vote at the Republican National Convention" (Jan. 21, 1976, 8). Jules Witcover's caucus story in the *Washington Post* mentioned neither the Republican meetings nor the straw poll (Jan. 21, 1976, A1, A4).

The weekly magazines devoted little space to the Republicans in Iowa. *Time*, in a story that gave 17 lines to the Republican and 130 to the Democratic caucuses, interpreted Ford's slim 45 to 43 percent victory in the straw poll as a setback for the president, thus placing Ford on the defensive in his bid for renomination (Feb. 2, 1976, 12, 17). The tone of the other magazines was similar. *Newsweek* thought the president would not find his slim victory in the Iowa straw poll "reassuring" (Feb. 2, 1976, 16), and *U.S. News and World Report* said: "President Gerald Ford may be in trouble" because of his "disappointingly small" margin in the poll (Feb. 2, 1976, 16).

The Republican caucus straw poll seems to have been a red flag for the media. It alerted those who thought that an incumbent president would have little trouble winning renomination against a challenger who was considered too ideological, and it confirmed the suspicion held by others that President Ford was in trouble. The Republican meetings did not receive nearly as much attention as their Democratic counterparts, but that undoubtedly was because their straw poll was unrelated to delegate selection. It was little more than a beauty contest. Iowa Governor Robert

Ray put it succinctly: "I don't think our caucuses hold quite the same meaning as the Democrats' " (*DMR* Jan. 20, 1976, 7A).

The 1976 Republican results drawn from the sixty-two sample precincts showed that participants cast 264 votes for Ford and 248 for Reagan. There were 62 votes categorized as undecided, and 9 votes were cast for other candidates. Apparently no results were obtained from at least one sample precinct. The *Des Moines Register* reported on January 20 that in a Polk County precinct selected for the survey, Delaware 2, nobody "showed up to unlock the door" (Jan. 20, 1976, 1A). The media interpretation that Reagan was a viable challenger was based on a sixteen-vote plurality among 583 Iowa Republicans. Such a poll may be very slim evidence for that judgment, but it again illustrates the media quest for reportable news about the progress of the campaign.

The Impact of the 1976 Caucuses

The year 1976 was a pivotal one for the Iowa caucuses. The state political parties worked very hard to attract the attention of the presidential candidates and the news media, including observing a common caucus date. The Republicans were disappointed that President Ford and Governor Reagan ignored the state, but the officials did succeed in attracting extensive postcaucus media coverage of their straw poll.

Perhaps no one worked harder to promote the caucuses than Tom Whitney. He initiated straw polls and made sure that the candidates and the media were aware of them and ultimately their outcomes; he provided speaking opportunities for the presidential hopefuls; he created a statewide reporting system and tabulation center so that the caucuses provided hard news; and he even interpreted the results of the 1976 precinct caucuses to make them more interesting and clear-cut. With a lot of chutzpah, Whitney turned the caucuses into a media event that attracted to Iowa at least nine presidential candidates and most of the major national print and broadcast media.

The Iowa political parties were very pleased with the result. They had become significant actors in the presidential nominating process, and the impact of the caucuses was far greater than the few votes Iowa controlled at the national conventions. The party leaders and staff were now consulted by presidential hopefuls and were sought after by the national media. The attention focused on the caucuses also served as an excellent party development tool, since potential workers and donors were identified early in the political season.

The new media event was, in fact, good for the people of the state as a whole. Iowans tend to suffer from feelings of inferiority about their state. Perhaps too many bad jokes about the cold winters or the tastes of the little old lady from Dubuque had left their mark on the average Iowan's psyche, but the national attention made people feel good about themselves and their state. Reporters sought the political views of everyday people, and the media picture that emerged of a clean, competitive political system gave Iowans some hope that one day people east of the Alleghenies might be able to distinguish between Iowa and Idaho.

The new status of the caucuses was also economically beneficial to the state. No reliable data are available for 1976, but the presidential campaigns rented cars, occupied hotel rooms, dined at restaurants, and spent money in Iowa for various and sundry services. Beyond this the reporters who followed the campaigns also made their contribution to the state's economy.

The 1976 Iowa caucuses also had a significant impact on the national nominating process. The great boost given the Carter campaign has already been discussed. Carter, unknown nationally before Iowa, became the media front-runner after the caucuses, a fact that was worth untold dollars in free coverage. Carter's national finance director, Joel McCleary, indicated that the campaign had put most of its organizational efforts into Iowa and New Hampshire and "had no structure after Florida; we had planned only for the short haul. After Florida, it was all *NBC*, *CBS*, and the *New York Times*." (Arterton 1978a, 6–7).

Iowa is a perfect state for a dark-horse candidate for the presidency. It is a small state whose political culture lends itself to limited-budget personal campaigning. Moreover, the potential of the Iowa caucuses as a media event was relatively unknown in 1976; thus they were of great surprise value to Carter. This would change after 1976 as the Iowa caucuses became nationally known. The Iowa media event would command the attention of presidential candidates in 1980.

In the 1976 presidential race, media attention increasingly focused on the early nominating events, and the media based their expectations for future contests on their outcomes. The game focus of the media led reporters to overemphasize the significance of the early electoral events and to overlook the unrepresentative nature of states like Iowa and New Hampshire. As Morris Udall observed, since the media placed so much emphasis on the early events, presidential candidates had to concentrate more of their efforts and campaign funds on them. The realization also spread among state parties that in order to maximize their influence on the presidential primary process, they would have to hold their primary events early in the season. The front-loading that followed would reach a new high in 1984, when seventeen states scheduled primaries or caucuses in the first twenty-two days of the nominating season (*Congressional Quarterly Weekly Report*, Dec. 10, 1983, 2605; hereafter cited as *CQ*).

The Defense of a
Media Event

Not everyone was pleased with the early precinct caucuses and their great impact on the presidential nominating process. Several states, undoubtedly envious of the status afforded Iowa and probably not pleased to see a small farm state that normally supports Republican presidential candidates playing a pivotal role in choosing the Democratic nominee, pressed for changes in party rules governing the Democratic nominating season.

When the legislators in the Iowa General Assembly learned that compression of the primary schedule was a possibility, they reacted to the perceived threat to their now-famous caucuses by enacting legislation that required that precinct caucuses be held no later than the second Monday in February in even-numbered years (Ia. Gen. Assem. 1978, chap. 1042, p. 207). Since national party rules governing primary processes take precedent over state laws, the legislative action was largely symbolic.

Although national party rules that compressed the Democratic nominating season into a thirteen-week period between the second Tuesday in March and the second Tuesday in June were enacted for 1980, Iowa's (and New Hampshire's) position of prominence was preserved by the inclusion of an appeals process for states that had held nominating events earlier in 1976 (Democratic National Committee, 1978). The Iowa Democrats requested and received a variance to hold their 1980 precinct caucuses in January, thus successfully parrying the attempt to limit their influence in the presidential nominating process.

References

Apple, R. W. 1975. "Carter Appears to Hold a Solid Lead in Iowa as the Campaign's First Test Approaches." *New York Times*, October 27, p. 17L.

———. 1976a. "Democratic Chiefs Beginning to Rate Presidential Rivals." *New York Times*, January 12, pp. 1, 19.

———. 1976b. "Carter Defeats Bayh by 2–1 in Iowa Vote; Many Uncommitted." *New York Times*, January 20, pp. 1, 20.

———. 1976c. "Carter Is Regarded as Getting Big Gain from Iowa Results." *New York Times*, January 21, pp. 1, 28.

Arterton, F. Christopher. 1978a. "Campaign Organizations Confront the Media-Political Environment." In *Race for the Presidency: The Media and the Nominating Process*, edited by James D. Barber, 3–25. Englewood Cliffs, N.J.: Prentice-Hall.

———. 1978b. "The Media Politics of Presidential Campaigns: A Study of the Carter Nomination Drive." In *Race for the Presidency: The Media and the Nominating Process*, edited by James D. Barber, 26–54. Englewood Cliffs, N.J.: Prentice-Hall.

Brown, Ralph. 1986. Telephone interview with author, April 23. Brown was the executive director of the Iowa Republican party from 1975 to 1977.

Congressional Quarterly Weekly Report. 1983.

Democratic National Committee. 1978. Delegate Selection Rules for the 1980 Democratic National Convention. Mimeographed.

Des Moines Register. 1976.

Flansburg, James. 1975a. "Carter Urges Withdrawal of Troops in Far East." *Des Moines Register*, February 27, p. 34.

———. 1975b. "Jimmy Carter: Iowans Find He's No Maddox." *Des Moines Register*, March 2, pp. 1, 6.

———. 1975c. "Democrats to Be Polled on Nominees." *Des Moines Register*, September 22, p. 1A.

———. 1975d. "8 Bring Presidential Campaigns to Iowa." *Des Moines Register*, October 25, p. 1A.

———. 1975e. "McGovern Challenges '76 Hopefuls." *Des Moines Register*, October 26, pp. 1A, 14A.

———. 1975f. "Carter Tops Democratic Straw Poll." *Des Moines Register*, October 27, p. 1A.

_____. 1976a. "Campaign '76: Issues Bow to Organization." *Des Moines Register*, January 4, pp. 1A, 16A.

_____. 1976b. "Reagan in D.M. to Rally Supporters." *Des Moines Register*, January 18, p. 5A.

_____. 1976c. "Parties Set for Caucuses in Iowa Tonight." *Des Moines Register*, January 19, pp. 1A, 7A.

_____. 1976d. "Demo Caucus Projections Misleading." *Des Moines Register*, January 25, pp. 1A, 5A.

Hollobaugh, Dix. 1976. "Rubbing Shoulders with the Media at $10 a Head." *Des Moines Register*, January 20, p. 7A.

Hunt, Albert R. 1976. "The Campaigning in Iowa Adds Up to Just About Zero." *Wall Street Journal*, January 15, pp. 1, 20.

Iowa. General Assembly. 1975–78. *Acts and Resolutions*. Des Moines: State of Iowa.

Iowa Democratic Party. 1980. Precinct Caucus Kit, 1980. Mimeographed.

Matthews, Donald R. 1978. "Winnowing." In *Race for the Presidency: The Media and the Nominating Process*, edited by James D. Barber, 55–78. Englewood Cliffs, N.J.: Prentice-Hall.

Newsweek. 1976.

Paletz, David L., and Robert M. Entman. 1981. *Media, Power, Politics*. New York: Free Press.

Robinson, Michael J. 1981. "The Media in 1980: Was the Message the Message?" In *The American Elections of 1980*, edited by Austin Ranney, 177–211. Washington, D.C.: American Enterprise Institute.

Robinson, Michael J., and Margaret A. Sheehan. 1983. *Over the Wire and on TV: CBS and UPI in Campaign '80*. New York: Russell Sage Foundation.

Roth, Luke. 1984. Telephone interview with author, December 7. Roth was the executive director of the Iowa Republican party from 1983 to 1985.

Schier, Steven E. 1980. *The Rules of the Game: Democratic National Convention Delegate Selection in Iowa and Wisconsin*. Washington, D.C.: University Press of America.

Schram, Martin. 1977. *Running for President 1976: The Carter Campaign*. New York: Stein and Day.

Steffen, J. P. 1984. Interview with author, December 4. Steffen has been the caucus chair of the Iowa Democratic party since 1983.

Time. 1976.

U.S. News and World Report. 1976.

Wall Street Journal. 1976.

Whitney, Tom. 1983. Telephone interview with author, March 17. Whitney was the chair of the Iowa Democratic party from 1973 to 1977.

_____. 1986. Written comments to author, June 5.

Witcover, Jules. 1976. "Iowa Victory Gives Carter Momentum." *Washington Post*, January 21, pp. A1, A4.

_____. 1977. *Marathon: The Pursuit of the Presidency, 1971–1976.* New York: Viking Press.

6

The 1980 Caucuses: A Media Event Becomes an Institution

The Iowa precinct caucuses were the opening round in the 1980 primary and caucus season. George McGovern's success in 1972 and Jimmy Carter's emergence as the Democratic front-runner in 1976 assured the caucuses of a position of prominence in the presidential nominating game. Iowa now rivaled New Hampshire for media attention, and as Ronald Reagan was to learn, the media expect all candidates to play the game in the early nominating contests. Most of the 1980 candidates realized that Iowa had become a significant part of the presidential race and committed their campaigns to major efforts in the precinct caucuses. George Bush explained his decision to mount a Carter-style campaign in Iowa this way: "The action begins in Iowa. It's where everything starts for everybody" (*Time* Jan. 21, 1980, 28).

Precaucus Activity

The candidates began their organizational efforts well in advance of the 1980 precinct caucuses. Although campaign expenses, particularly media costs, are relatively low in Iowa, media campaigns tend to yield few results. Success in a caucus state is largely dependent on good grass-roots organizing. As one county supervisor put it: "You've got to turn folks out for four hours on the coldest night of the year to fight with their neighbors about politics" (*Newsweek* Nov. 26, 1979, 58). The task is complicated by the dispersion of the population. The state's 2.9 million people are spread throughout ninety-nine counties, with few major population centers. Moreover, organizational efforts at the county level must be targeted to those individuals most likely to attend precinct caucuses. Pinpointing, contacting, and winning the allegiance of Democratic and Republican activists, who represent a small percentage of all registered partisans, require excellent organizational skills.

The successful 1980 Iowa campaigns of Jimmy Carter and George Bush again demonstrated this point. Both spent months putting together their organizations. John Connally and Howard Baker, on the other hand, had little organization in Iowa and invested heavily in media time in hopes of increasing the caucus participation of their supporters. Their efforts yielded few positive results (*Time* Jan. 21, 1980, 30).

The Republican Campaign.   On the basis of much soft evidence, the news media concluded that Ronald Reagan was the early front-runner for the Republican nomination. He was a campaign veteran, was well organized, was strong in the national polls, had a firm base of support within the party, and had access to money (Jones 1981, 73). He was also judged to be the front-runner in Iowa, a position he retained throughout the caucus campaign (*CQ* Jan. 12, 1980, 85). Reagan had worked in Des Moines as a sports announcer for WHO radio in his early professional years, which made him something of a "favorite son" candidate. He had challenged President Ford in 1976, and his strong showing in the Iowa caucus straw poll was the first evidence that Ford was vulnerable. Subsequently he came very close to wresting the Republican nomination from an incumbent president. Additionally, an August 1979 statewide *Des Moines Register* poll indicated strong support for Reagan among the Iowa rank and file. In that poll 48 percent of the respondents favored Reagan, 23 percent Baker, 11 percent Connally, 4 percent Dole, 2 percent Crane, and 1 percent each Anderson, Bush, and others. Nine percent of the respondents were undecided (*Iowa Poll: 1979*, poll no. 952).

As the front-runner, Reagan adopted an early strategy of remaining "above" the campaign. He refused to appear at forums with other Republican candidates, asserting that the debate was with the Democrats, not with members of his own party. Pursuing this strategy in Iowa, his aides developed, at great expense, a significant campaign organization, but the candidate himself campaigned only four times in the state.

George Bush spent the better part of a year campaigning in Iowa. During that period he made thirty-one visits to the state (Roberts 1984), and one of his sons even resided in Iowa for a time in the fall of 1979. Although the August Iowa Poll indicated that Bush was largely unknown to the rank and file, he spent his time cultivating the support of party activists and local leaders (*CQ* Jan. 12, 1980, 85). These were the people most likely to attend the precinct caucuses, and by January Bush was the best organized of the Republicans. *Time* magazine reported that he had eighteen full-time and eighty part-time workers in the state, had pinpointed the voters most likely to attend the caucuses, and had secured "more endorsements than any of his rivals." The story went on to say that there were "indications that he has strength in the state's more populated areas" (Jan. 21, 1980, 30). Bush needed to do better than expected in Iowa to establish himself as a viable challenger to Reagan.

The other Republican hopefuls—Senator Howard Baker, former Texas governor John Connally, Senator Robert Dole, Congressman Philip Crane, and Congressman John Anderson—conducted Iowa campaigns of varied quality. Connally and Baker made serious efforts but never attained the high levels of organization accomplished by Reagan and Bush. Baker did receive the endorsement of the influential Iowa State Education Association and some late help from Governor Robert Ray, but although helpful, this did not make up for his lack of organization. The Baker and Connally campaigns, characterized by frequent personal visits and large media expenditures as the caucuses neared, were probably better suited for primary elections than precinct caucuses (*Time* Jan. 21, 1980, 30). Dole and Crane failed to develop effective organizations even though Crane visited Iowa thirty times during the campaign (Roberts 1984), and they never emerged from the ranks of the also-rans. Anderson made little effort in Iowa.

To stimulate interest in their caucuses, the Iowa Republicans employed the tactic used so successfully by the Democrats in 1976: They conducted a presidential preference straw poll at every opportunity. The results of these polls were consistently reported by the *Des Moines Register*, and some found their way into the national media. Bush's organizational efforts began to pay dividends in the form of victories in these polls. In one taken at a May Republican fund-raiser featuring Henry Kissinger, Bush surprised news pundits by outpacing Reagan 40 to 26 percent (Germond and Witcover 1979a, 10A). At an October 11 Republican fund-raiser in the Second Congressional District, Bush outdistanced the field with 166 votes. His nearest competitor, Connally, with 93 votes, was followed by Crane, with 73 votes, and then Reagan and Baker, who had 44 votes each (Yepsen 1979a, 6A).

It is interesting that these polls of party activists occurred on either side of the August Iowa Poll that showed that only 1 percent of the Iowa Republican rank and file favored Bush. Although largely unknown to most Iowans, Bush was making headway where it counted, among those likely to attend the caucuses. This clearly illustrated the danger of making too much of public opinion polls in a caucus state, since only a small fraction of the partisans attend caucuses. Attempting to extrapolate the preferences of a small group of party activists from a large sample of the rank and file is doomed to failure, and the results can be very misleading. Nonetheless, the results of the August Iowa Poll, and subsequent December and January samplings, were reported nationally, presumably to give the country an indication of the status of the presidential campaign in Iowa.

The most significant Republican event of the fall, and the fifth event to conduct a preference poll, was the October 13 fund-raising dinner in Ames. Reminiscent of the 1976 Democratic Jefferson-Jackson Day dinner, the Iowa Republican party invited all the Republican presidential candidates to the fifty-dollar-a-plate dinner, the purpose of which was to retire the party's 1978 campaign debt (Flansburg 1979a, 4A). Nine candidates of varying stature—Anderson, Baker, Bush, Connally, Crane, Dole, California businessman Ben Fernandez, South Dakota senator Larry Pressler, and perennial candidate Harold Stassen of Minnesota—participated and drew 3500 Iowans to the event (Flansburg, Yepsen,and Pedersen 1979, 1A). The candidates were each permitted eight minutes for speeches and were given "campaign booths" on the floor of the hall. Notably absent was Ronald Reagan, whose official reason for declining the invitation was to avoid fostering disharmony within the party. A more plausible explanation for Reagan's failure to appear was his front-runner status and the desire not to share a platform with the less well known Republicans (Flansburg, Pedersen, and Yepsen 1979, 1A, 4A).

The Ames fund-raiser was another plus for the Bush candidacy in Iowa. He drew the largest applause during the introduction of candidates (Flansburg, Yepsen, and Pedersen, 1979, 1A), and he was an easy winner in the straw poll, with 36 percent of the 1454 votes cast. Reagan, with 11 percent of the vote, was a distant fourth behind Connally and Dole, with 15 percent each.

Copyright 1979, Des Moines Register and Tribune Company.

Ronald Reagan was the odds-on favorite to win the Republican presidential nomination in 1980 and he chose to limit his appearances in Iowa and not to appear at campaign functions with other Republican candidates. Reagan's strategy of non-involvement was resented by Iowans, and they dealt his campaign a setback by supporting George Bush in the Republican caucus poll. After the Iowa defeat, Reagan changed his campaign strategy and began appearing with fellow Republicans.

George Bush won a sixth straight preference poll two weeks later at a Story County fund-raising event, leading the *Register*'s political reporters to conclude that Reagan's "campaign may be in deep trouble in Iowa" (Flansburg and Yepsen 1979, 1A, 13A). Jack Germond and Jules Witcover, picking up on the *Register* articles, alerted the nation in a syndicated column that the Reagan strategy of noninvolvement could be hurting his chances in Iowa (1979b, 10A).

Shortly after the Ames dinner the *Register* announced that it would hold a debate for Republican presidential candidates in Des Moines on January 5 and that invitations had been extended to the seven candidates then conducting campaigns in Iowa—Anderson, Baker, Bush, Connally, Crane, Dole, and Reagan. A Democratic debate between Carter and Kennedy was scheduled for January 7, and when all the invited candidates of both parties, except Reagan, accepted the invitations, the television networks decided to provide live coverage of both debates (Graham 1979, 4A).

The late fall was a time of intense campaign activity by the Republican hopefuls in Iowa. The Baker campaign received the endorsement of Iowa teachers and help from Governor Ray, and that helped to compensate for his lack of organization. Connally attempted to keep his campaign visible by purchasing extensive television time. The other candidates, including Reagan, appeared more frequently in the state, and Reagan, at a December 14 fund-raiser in the Fifth Congressional District, claimed party unity as the reason he would not take part in the upcoming *Register* debate (Flansburg 1979b, 16A). Bush continued to make organizational inroads, and a December Iowa Poll found that twice as many people said they had been contacted by Bush as by any other candidate (*Iowa Poll: 1979*, poll no. 959).

In Iran, student terrorists seized the United States embassy in early November, but this had little immediate impact on the Republican campaign, since the candidates chose not to make the ensuing hostage crisis an issue. Later, however, as the nation rallied around President Carter, Iran had a great effect on the campaign. The president's standing in national public opinion surveys soared, and as it did he became less and less inclined to engage in political dialogue. On December 28, Carter withdrew from the Des Moines presidential debate, announcing that he would not campaign outside Washington for the duration of the hostage crisis. Neither the Republicans nor the press liked the president's decision, and the media let it be known on several occasions (Flansburg 1979c, 1A). The Democratic debate was canceled, and shortly thereafter the networks announced that they no longer planned live television coverage of the Republican debate.

Nevertheless, the Republican debate, minus live TV coverage and Ronald Reagan, went on as scheduled in the Des Moines Civic Center, with six presidential hopefuls, a panel of distinguished journalists, approximately 200 reporters, and over 2000 Iowans in attendance. The candidates, in addition to addressing one another, took turns admonishing Reagan for his absence (Pedersen 1980, 1A, 5A; Flansburg, Risser, and Graham 1980, 1A, 4A). The debate was well received by news reporters, although there was no clear winner, and the *New York Times* called it "surprisingly interesting and revealing" (Jan. 7, 1980, A18). Reporters were uniformly critical of Reagan for failing to participate in the discussion, and so were Iowans; Reagan's share in the Iowa Poll standings plunged from 50 percent in early December to 26 percent the day after the Republican debate (*Iowa Poll: 1980*, poll no. 969).

The Democratic Campaign.   An incumbent president usually does not have to endure a primary battle, but in 1980 for the second consecutive election a sitting president was challenged for his party's nomination. Ted Kennedy brought his famous name and considerable family to Iowa to contest the Democratic precinct caucuses in 1980, and in the process he assured the Democratic meetings of a great deal of media attention. After suffering a loss to President Carter in the Florida county caucuses in mid-October, the senator downplayed the importance of that event and announced that the Iowa caucuses would be the first "true test" of his challenge to

After an early loss to President Carter in the 1979 Florida county caucuses, Ted Kennedy decided to stake his presidential hopes on the Iowa precinct caucuses. He announced that Iowa would provide the first real test of his challenge to the Carter presidency. Later he would regret placing so much emphasis on the Iowa meetings.

Carter (*DMR* Oct. 14, 1979, 2A). After a late start, he pursued Iowa delegates by personally campaigning in the state for a total of about twenty days, including one six-day stint in January, and by importing his mother, sisters, and many other members of the Kennedy clan to campaign for him (Flansburg 1980a, 1B, 3B).

Carter, on the other hand, did not visit Iowa, because of the Iranian hostage crisis, but he certainly did not ignore the state that had made him the Democratic front-runner in 1976. Rosalynn Carter and Vice-President Mondale were frequent visitors, and a long list of surrogates made their way to Iowa to campaign for the president. Additionally, Carter used the traditional advantages of incumbency—international crises, the awarding of grants, and invitations to Washington—to his advantage. In October about 200 Iowans visited the White House for a day of briefings, and it was not uncommon for Iowa Democrats to answer their phones in the months before the precinct caucuses and discover that the caller was the President of the United States. Moreover, Carter understood the nature of organizational politics in a caucus state, and with adequate financial resources, a paid campaign staff of twenty-one people was functioning in Iowa fully nine months before the caucuses (Flansburg and Pedersen 1979, 1A, 5A). He also had the support of the state Democratic establishment—the state chair and most county chairs—and the politically potent Iowa State Education Association (*CQ* Jan. 12, 1980, 84). By the time Kennedy entered the race, Carter was well organized throughout the state.

A third Democratic candidate, Governor Jerry Brown of California, emerged after the *Register* announced the Democratic debate and he demanded to be included (*DMR* Nov. 12, 1979, 3A). Brown spent a total of six days in Iowa, and in a late November visit he opened a state campaign headquarters in an attempt to persuade the *Register* editorial staff that he intended to mount a serious campaign in the state. The effort was successful, and in early December the *Register* invited Brown to participate in the January 7

Democratic debate (Leavitt 1979, 1A). It is apparent that Brown was only interested in the potential media exposure afforded by the debate, since he did not seriously contest Iowa, and on January 16 he announced his withdrawal from the caucus contests and urged his supporters to run as uncommitted delegates (Flansburg 1980b, 1A).

The Democrats conducted fewer polls in 1979 and 1980 than did the Republicans, primarily because Ted Kennedy did not enter the contest until early November. The first major encounter was a preference poll taken at the November 3 Jefferson-Jackson Day dinner in Ames. A similar poll four years earlier had given the nation the first hint of Carter's organizational strength in Iowa. With the president in self-imposed exile in the White House, the keynote speaker was Vice-President Mondale. Not to be outdone, the Kennedy campaign imported Bobby's widow, Ethel Kennedy, and son Joseph for the event.

Kennedy attempted to persuade the media, however, that he had little chance of doing well in the Ames poll because of his late start in the state and the far superior Carter organization. His position was complicated somewhat by the August Iowa Poll that showed Kennedy holding a commanding 49 percent to 26 percent lead over Carter among the Democratic rank and file (*Iowa Poll: 1979*, poll no. 947). It is possible that the August poll raised expectations among Kennedy supporters and the media, since it made Kennedy appear more viable than he was at the time. As of early November, Kennedy had little organization in Iowa, whereas the Carter campaign had been in place for seven months. The Kennedy people were not playing the expectations game with their prediction; they had been out-organized and knew it.

The Jefferson-Jackson Day dinner is normally the big Democratic event of the year, and 1979 was no exception. Some 2800 people paid thirty dollars each to attend the fund-raiser and hear Vice-President Mondale make the case for Carter's reelection, and to have the opportunity to cast a ballot in the straw poll conducted by the Iowa Daily

Press Association (Pedersen, Flansburg, and Yepsen 1979, 1A, 12A). The event did not, however, approach the circuslike atmosphere of the 1976 Democratic dinner.

Kennedy was correct in attempting to downplay the Ames straw poll. Carter was the overwhelming winner, with 71 percent of the 2320 participants favoring his candidacy and only 26 percent supporting Kennedy. The margin of victory was so great that Carter aide Bill Romjue felt it necessary to issue his own disclaimer. He contended that Carter was not as strong statewide as indicated by the poll and that the victory margin should not be taken too seriously, given that Kennedy was just starting to organize in Iowa. The media tended to agree with Romjue's assessment and largely discounted the results of the Jefferson-Jackson Day poll (Yepsen 1979b, 3A).

As December approached, Kennedy moved his Iowa campaign into high gear. There was self-imposed pressure to do well in the caucuses since he had dubbed Iowa the first "true test," and now he had to deliver or face a negative media interpretation due to the expectations he had helped to create. He made a strong effort in the final three months before the caucuses, concentrating on the major urban areas, and with the help of organized labor he "created an organization considered to be one of the finest ever seen in Iowa" (CQ Jan. 12, 1980, 84). From an anecdotal standpoint, it is interesting that as Kennedy and his extended family intensified their efforts in Iowa, the senator's poll standing vis-à-vis Jimmy Carter dropped dramatically. The December Iowa Poll showed each commanding the allegiance of 40 percent of the Iowa Democrats. Iran was negating his campaign efforts, at least with the rank and file.

Another casualty of the president's soaring popularity in the public opinion polls, as previously noted, was the Democratic presidential debate arranged by the *Des Moines Register*. News organizations all over the country condemned Carter's decision not to participate (*DMR* Jan. 5, 1980, 10A), and James Flansburg asserted that "the

Carter record clearly shows that he doesn't debate his political opponents when he believes he's ahead of them"
(1979d, 2C). Whatever the reason, the subsequent cancel-
lation of the Democratic debate pulled the plug on live
network television coverage for the Republican debate on
January 7 and on Brown's Iowa campaign. The action also
left Kennedy sparring with a shadow for the support of the
Iowa Democrats.

The 1980 Precinct Caucuses

The candidates, and Carter's surrogates,
practically lived in Iowa the final week of the campaign.
Kennedy, Bush, Connally, Baker, Dole, Crane, and even
Ronald Reagan attempted by personal contact to win
caucus support. It had been a vigorous campaign, and six
candidates (Connally invested heavily in television time
and may have outspent each of the other candidates) spent
close to the federal limit on their campaigns. The figures in
Table 6.1 probably understate total campaign spending, as
candidates were known to record Iowa expenses elsewhere
by renting cars, for example, in bordering states like Ne-
braska. The institutionalization of the precinct caucuses
increased their costs considerably. In 1976 Jimmy Carter
had spent less than $100,000 en route to his media victory
in Iowa (*CQ* Dec. 10, 1983, 2601).

Media Coverage. Media coverage of the
1980 caucuses was immense. The major national print
and broadcast media were represented in Iowa by about
300 reporters and technicians, and unlike 1976, when, to
be available for TV interviews, Jimmy Carter had to be in
New York on the night of the caucuses, the three television
networks set up temporary studios in Iowa. On January
21, the day of the caucuses, NBC's "Today" show and all

Table 6.1. 1980 Candidate Precaucus Expenditures in Iowa

	Total expenditure
Brown	$ 30,330
Carter	493,067
Kennedy	442,858
Anderson	1,233
Baker	480,951
Bush	462,382
Crane	102,844
Dole	227,636
Reagan	466,088

Source: Data are from the Federal Election Commission report *FEC Reports on Financial Activity, 1979–80: Final Report, Presidential Pre-Nomination Campaigns,* Table A8. Connally is not included since he did not accept federal money and therefore was not required to file a report. He also was not bound by the Iowa spending limit of $489,882.

three network evening news programs originated from Des Moines (Hainey 1980, 5A).

A systematic examination of the election stories aired by the "CBS Evening News" during a twelve-month period from July 1, 1979, through June 30, 1980, indicates that coverage of the precinct caucuses increased dramatically from 1976 to 1980 and that by 1980 Iowa had replaced New Hampshire as the foremost media event of the presidential nominating season. Robinson and Sheehan had reached the opposite conclusion, that New Hampshire prevailed over Iowa as the most reported nominating event of the presidential campaign (1983, 174–81). Their conclusion was based on an analysis of CBS News and UPI stories, but for only a six-month period from January 1 to June 6, 1980. The Iowa caucuses were held in January in both 1976 and 1980, and by not examining the longer period before the 1980 caucuses analyzed here, Robinson and Sheehan missed many of the Iowa and New Hampshire reports aired by CBS News.

Table 6.2 compares CBS's 1975–76 and 1979–80 coverage of the Iowa precinct caucuses with the New Hampshire primary election for the one-year period from July 1 to June 30. The number of Iowa stories aired by CBS increased from 13 in 1976 to 54 in 1980. The number of New Hampshire primary election stories, on the other hand, declined slightly from 44 in 1976 to 40 in 1980, indicating a proportional increase in Iowa stories rather than a general increase in coverage of the 1980 nominating process. It is apparent that spirited contests in both parties piqued media interest in the precinct caucuses. The early date made Iowa more attractive, at least to CBS News, and reporters were willing to ignore the fact that the results produced in Iowa were considerably softer than the "hard news" produced by the New Hampshire primary election.

Table 6.2. 1976 and 1980 CBS News Stories on Iowa and New Hampshire

	July 1, 1975–June 30, 1976			July 1, 1979–June 30, 1980		
	Weekday	Weekend	Total	Weekday	Weekend	Total
Iowa	12	1	13	37	17	54
N.H.	40	4	44	29	11	40

Source: Data from the *Television News Index and Abstracts*, produced by Vanderbilt University. All evening broadcasts during the two twelve-month periods were reviewed. Stories were counted that related the two events to the national primary race or that described candidates' visits to one of the states. Two or more story headings on the same day were recorded as separate entities. If a story included both Iowa and New Hampshire, it was listed under the tally of both states. Finally, the weekend information is incomplete due to the absence of some weekends from the abstracts.

The early and sustained attention given the 1980 caucuses also stimulated citizen interest, and officials reported record levels of participation throughout the state. The Republican poll indicated that 106,000 persons had participated, and the Democrats estimated that 100,000 people had attended their meetings. The large turnout included many political amateurs attending their first caucus, and some of the usually well orchestrated events degenerated into rather chaotic affairs. Organizational efforts faltered as meetings spilled over into second and third rooms, and supplies ranging from registration forms to ballots were in short supply (Bullard and Kneeland 1980, 1B).

The results of large-scale citizen participation produced mixed results. Many meetings elected people who were attending their first caucus to be delegates to county conventions, and others were examples of only symbolic democracy, because citizens unfamiliar with caucus procedures had little impact. An interesting example of the latter occurred in Republican caucus 74 in Des Moines, where 474 people attended and participated in the straw poll, but upon completion of the poll approximately half of those present left, before the real business of delegate selection took place (Bittick 1980).

The Republican Caucuses.   The 1980 Republican caucuses shared fully in the media attention previously dominated by the Democratic meetings. To accommodate the media's need for results, the Iowa Republican party, which does not compile delegate counts, asked all precincts to conduct a preference poll of those in attendance, although the final decision to participate in what Adam Clymer of the *New York Times* called "the biggest straw poll yet" remained with individual caucuses (1980a, 4C). The straw poll was unrelated to delegate selection.

The Reagan camp still expected a victory in Iowa, but the signs were everywhere that a Bush upset was in the making. The string of straw-poll victories indicated a solid Bush organization, and reports had surfaced that he would do well in both the first and second congressional districts (Pedersen and Yepsen 1980, 1A, 3A). Reporters attended caucuses to gain a flavor of the process, and most precincts conducted the straw poll. Table 6.3 reports the outcome of the Republican preference poll. The contest was very close, with George Bush emerging only 2 percentage points ahead of Ronald Reagan.

Although the closeness of the contest was widely re-

Table 6.3. 1980 Republican Caucus Straw Poll Results

	Preferences	Percentage of total votes
Bush	33,530	31.6
Reagan	31,348	29.5
Baker	16,216	15.3
Connally	9,861	9.3
Crane	7,135	6.7
Anderson	4,585	4.3
Undecided	1,800	1.7
Dole	1,576	1.5
	106,051	99.9

Source: Data from official results provided by the Iowa Republican party. They represent 2,389 of 2,531 precincts (94.4%). A total of 142 precincts did not hold caucuses, did not conduct the poll, or simply did not report their results. These results were reported in *Newsweek*, *Time*, and *U.S. News and World Report*. The print and broadcast media reported less complete results that had Bush leading Reagan by 4 to 6 percentage points.

ported, it was secondary to the fact that Bush had won. The media trumpeted his victory around the nation. Bush's picture was on the cover of *Newsweek*, and an accompanying headline declared: "Bush Breaks Out of the Pack." An eight-page story on the Republican caucuses called Iowa "the first major test of the 1980 Presidential campaign" and stated that "Bush collected an impressive 31.5 percent of the vote." The story included twelve pictures of Republican candidates, ten of Bush and one each of Reagan and Howard Baker, who finished second and third respectively (*Newsweek* Feb. 4, 1980, 30, 31, 33, 35–38).

The *Washington Post* declared that Bush had "established himself tonight as a serious challenger to Ronald Reagan by running neck-and-neck with the former California governor in the Iowa precinct caucuses" (Peterson 1980, A1). Two days after the caucuses, a *Post* editorial called Bush's win an impressive victory and a "major setback" for Reagan (Jan. 23, 1980, A22).

A *Wall Street Journal* headline read: "Carter and Bush Win 1st Round but Have No Knockdowns Yet." The story went on to explain that Bush had upset Reagan, "whose first name has been front-runner for the past year" and concluded that as a result, Reagan needed a win in New Hampshire to remain a credible contender for the Republican nomination (Perry and Hunt 1980, 1, 37).

The *New York Times* concluded that "Mr. Bush's unexpected comfortable victory and the failures of others suddenly made the Republican race more of a two-man contest," thus reducing the remaining five Republican candidates to the status of also-rans after only one primary event (Clymer 1980c, A1). After two days as part of the George Bush media chorus, the *New York Times* published an editorial entitled "Apples and Oranges in Iowa," in which they placed the Iowa caucuses in perspective. It noted that the caucuses were not a primary election and that Bush's victory was in a straw poll of caucus members held before, and unrelated to, the selection of delegates to county conventions (Jan. 23, 1980, A22). The editorial did little, however, to change the impact of the caucuses: Bush's star rose dramatically after Iowa. A February 1980 CBS News–*New York Times* Poll showed that support for Bush among national Republicans had grown from 6 to 24 percent in less than thirty days (Robinson 1981, 203).

It is clear that Bush's win in Iowa was a media victory. He exceeded media expectations and reaped the publicity. Robinson called Bush's "big" victory in Iowa one of the major medialities of the 1980 presidential campaign (1981, 196). Actually, the Bush margin of victory was anything but big—a plurality of just over 2,000 out of 106,000 votes—and it was in an essentially meaningless beauty contest conducted for the media. Moreover, Robinson documents that even though the national media elevated Bush to the position of major contender, he never seriously threatened Reagan for the Republican nomination. (Bush's standing among Republicans after the Iowa caucuses is discussed in Robinson 1981, 203.)

Media events, however, take on a life of their own and affect political campaigns. Iowa forced Reagan to abandon the campaign strategy of ignoring the Republican opposition, and he mounted a full-blown campaign in New Hampshire. Bush may never have seriously threatened Reagan's bid for the Republican nomination, but the media brouhaha generated by the Iowa caucuses gave him sufficient momentum to make him the vice-presidential nominee.

By the time that the thirty-seven Republican delegates were finally selected at the district and state conventions in June, Reagan followers were in control and Bush was no longer a candidate for the presidency. He was, however, running hard for the vice-presidential nomination, and in an appearance at the Republican state convention he pledged his support to Ronald Reagan and made a plea for party unity (Flansburg and Yepsen 1980a, 1A, 4A).

The Validity of the Republican Results. The 1980 poll, unlike the 1976 effort, which included only sixty-two sample precincts, was held on a statewide basis, and with 2531 precincts, the logistics of the endeavor were complex. Party officials set up a tabulation center at the Hotel Ft. Des Moines that included Apple computers and card readers, a bank of telephones, and volunteers staffing the system. Each of the precincts reported by phone directly to Des Moines, and that proved to be the first flaw in the system. Then those receiving the precinct data penciled in the poll results on computer cards and fed them into the card readers, and that was the second weak point of the system. Almost immediately the tabulators fell behind due to the volume of data, then problems developed with the card readers, and one of the computers (indeed, the system in general) was very slow. Reporters, facing deadlines, were angry about the lack of results. Party officials agree that it would have been more practical to have county party workers collect precinct data and report the numbers to the state tabulation center, thus reducing the Des Moines callers from 2531 to 99, but the idea had been rejected by the state central committee. When the card readers failed to work properly, the system began to come apart (Hyde July 3, 1986; Bonsignoir 1986).

When the system's failure became apparent, one of the party officials supervising the project thought it best to call a press conference to inform the reporters of the fact. The more senior of the two party workers overseeing the counting disagreed, and the job of completing the counting by hand continued into the early-morning hours (Hyde July 3, 1986). During that time it became apparent that some of the totals on the large results board were strange. CBS officials thought the numbers from six counties were too large and favored Bush by too great a margin (Mitofsky 1986). There were also "patterns of error" from the Fifth Congressional District—with more precincts reporting than there were precincts—and at least one party official thought there were some "shenanigans" going on there (Hyde July 3, 1986). At that point, party workers moved the tabulation process from the hotel ballroom to state party headquarters, and with calculators rather than computers, they recounted, or at least spot-checked, all results. Incomplete data from some precincts led to inquiring phone calls and "extrapolations" by those doing the counting. The final results, completed on Tuesday afternoon, showed Bush and Reagan as separated by a margin of only 2 percent rather than the 4 to 6 percent spread reported in the newspapers the day after the caucuses. Based on sample precincts, CBS had it even closer—less than 1 percent separating the two candidates, with Reagan leading—and decided the race was too close to call. NBC had projected Bush as the winner (Plissner July 7, 1986).

It is clear from interviews with those present that the 1980 Iowa Republican tabulation system left much to be desired and that the party was unable to complete an accurate and reliable count of the results of its preference poll. Party officials assert that it was simply a case of their first attempt at a statewide reporting system not being up to the job. They are satisfied that they ultimately reported the most accurate figures possible from the available data, and they note that neither the Bush nor the Reagan people protested the results (Hyde July 3, 1986). Still, the candidacy of George Bush was given a tremendous boost by the media perception that he had upset Ronald Reagan in the Iowa precinct caucuses, and it is very troublesome to think that the media perception was based on incomplete and perhaps erroneous results. Bush may well have been the victor in the Iowa Republican straw poll, but even those doing the counting that night admit that we shall never know for sure, because of the problems encountered at the tabulation center.

Newspeople who were aware of the "results problem" were very disturbed that the poll figures they had reported may not have been accurate (Yepsen 1986; Plissner July 7, 1986). When combined with the problems with the 1976 Democratic results, this made two straight caucus seasons in which results given to the news media had been of questionable validity, and the newspeople wanted an independent body to provide caucus results in the future. Various media organizations put pressure on the Iowa Democrats in 1984 to cooperate and to allow the News Election Service to record the candidate preference of those attending caucuses after the first division into preference groups. (This effort is more thoroughly discussed in the next chapter.)

As noted in Chapter 5, there are no laws in Iowa governing the reporting of caucus results. Each party, without independent supervision, has developed a reporting system that purports to represent the outcomes of their respective processes. Reporters, and the nation, are asked to accept the validity, reliability, and honesty of the systems, but without independent judges this requires an act of faith. The reporting systems are complicated, and with the stakes so high, the possibility of error or fraud in an unregulated process exists. Iowa's political parties should be required to provide independently verified caucus results, or the media should ignore the state and its precinct caucuses.

The Democratic Caucuses.   On January 21 perhaps the most unusual straw poll of the primary season was held in Emmetsburg, a town in northwest Iowa that had become famous for voting for the winning candidate in presidential elections. A local radio station and the town's public works department cooperated to hold the "Cess Poll." KEMB-FM, broadcasting from the city water plant, reported how much the water level dropped in the town's water tower after residents flushed their toilets successively for Carter, Kennedy, and "undecided/don't care." The winner by a two-to-one margin was "undecided/don't care," followed by Carter, with Kennedy a distant third. The station concluded that Kennedy was "in deep water" in Emmetsburg (*DMR* Jan. 22, 1980, 1A).

The Democratic meetings were as lively as their Republican counterparts. A notable difference, however, was in media preparation for the Democratic caucuses. CBS selected ninety precincts and interviewed caucus participants as they arrived for the meetings. On that basis, at 8:51 P.M., before any delegate totals were posted at tabulation headquarters in Des Moines, CBS projected that Carter would defeat Kennedy by "better than 2–1" (Hainey 1980, 5A). (The early projections grew into a controversy in 1984 that is discussed in Chapter 7.)

Ultimately, President Carter outpolled Kennedy by a two-to-one margin in the delegate equivalents, reported in Table 6.4. The media interpretation of the Democratic caucus results was uniform: Carter had won a major vic-

Table 6.4.   1980 Democratic Precinct Caucus Results

	State delegate equivalents (%)
Carter	59.1
Kennedy	31.2
Uncommitted	9.6

Source: Data from official results provided by the Iowa Democratic party, based on 96 percent of the 2531 precincts. In 1980 the national delegate equivalents were downplayed by the party.

tory and Kennedy had been badly damaged. The *New York Times*, for example, declared, "Carter Wins Strong Victory in Iowa" (Clymer 1980b, A1), and a day later stated, "Victory by Carter Staggers Kennedy and Leaves His Campaign in Doubt" (Smith, 1980, A17).

The *Washington Post* story said that "President Carter dealt Sen. Edward M. Kennedy a decisive setback tonight" and concluded that the unusually small number of uncommitted delegates also was a setback for Jerry Brown, who had asked his followers to support uncommitted slates in the caucuses. Playing the expectations game, the story concluded that "Carter's landslide was worse than Kennedy expected." Finally, the writer thought that "Carter's victory was a vindication both of his strategy and his national leadership" (Broder 1980, A1, A4).

Whereas the *Post* story credited Iowa with mortally wounding Kennedy and vindicating the policies of President Carter, the *Wall Street Journal*, although it, too, played the expectations game, was considerably more restrained in its interpretation of the outcome of the precinct caucuses. The *Journal* story said that "Carter's overwhelming victory exceeded the White House's fondest hopes," and that Kennedy was "humiliated" because "no Kennedy has ever lost so badly." The *Journal*, however, did refer to the precinct caucuses as the first round of the 1980 primary season, and the story headline stated that there were "No Knockdowns Yet" (Perry and Hunt 1980, 1, 37). The *Christian Science Monitor* presented one of the few balanced and unsensational interpretations of both parties' caucus results in Iowa (Sperling 1980, 1, 10).

The *Newsweek* headline, on the other hand, asked, "Can Kennedy Hang On?" The three-page story used interesting rhetoric to describe the Iowa Democratic outcomes, asserting that the president had made good on his promise to "whip his ass" as he "buried the Senator and the twenty-year legend of Kennedy invincibility." Kennedy, it said, had been "engulfed by a tidal-wave turnout that made the caucuses the moral equivalent of a primary," and the margin of victory had been "big and persuasive enough to propel Carter to within dreaming distance of stitching up his renomination before the winter is out" (*Newsweek* Feb. 4, 1980, 43, 44, 49).

Kennedy did hang on all the way to the Democratic National Convention, but the media interpretation of the Iowa caucuses was very damaging to his campaign. Iowa had demonstrated to the media's satisfaction that Kennedy was not a viable threat to the Carter presidency, and it had proved to be a major step in the battle for the Democratic nomination.

Unlike 1972 and 1976, the two-to-one margin of delegate support for President Carter over Senator Kennedy held throughout the sequence of county, district, and state conventions in Iowa. The Iowa delegation to the 1980 national convention in New York included 31 delegates for Carter, 17 for Kennedy, and 2 uncommitted (Flansburg and Yepsen 1980b, 1A).

The Impact of the 1980 Precinct Caucuses

The precinct caucuses were institutionalized as part of the presidential nominating process in 1980. Iowa came to be well known as an important early nominating event, and as Reagan discovered, the media expected serious candidates to enter the contest. Several presidential hopefuls from both parties made all-out efforts in Iowa, and "surprise campaigns" like those of McGovern in 1972 and Carter in 1976 were no longer possible. The media might find the eventual winner in the precinct caucuses a surprise, but Iowa had become an early source of hard news about the progress of the presidential campaign, and both the candidates and the media were there in large numbers.

Iowa party leaders, businesspeople, and just plain citi-

zens greatly enjoyed and appreciated the notoriety of the
Iowa media event. The state's small population had previously limited the influence of the Iowa parties at the national conventions. Now Iowa "made" and "broke" presidential candidacies; the state's parties were significant
actors in the presidential nominating game.

Although it is impossible to gain access to reliable figures, the campaigns and those who follow and report on
them spent millions of dollars in Iowa in 1980, just as they
had in 1976. The capital city of Des Moines and its business community were probably the chief beneficiaries of
the financial infusion, and they did their best to support
the caucuses. The Des Moines Chamber of Commerce
worked hand in hand with the Iowa Republican and Democratic parties to promote the event.

Iowans in general seemed to enjoy the excitement associated with the precinct caucuses. It required little initia-
tive on the part of average citizens to see, hear, and shake
hands with presidential candidates, an occurrence that
was extremely rare prior to 1976. There were Iowans who
could now brag to their friends and relatives that a presidential candidate had visited or, in the case of Carter in
1976, slept in their homes. Others received telephone calls
from the president. Additionally, the caucuses and the national attention provided a break in the long, cold Iowa
winter.

The 1980 precinct caucuses, like those four years earlier, had a great impact on the presidential race. Ted Kennedy was seriously damaged by the media interpretation
that his campaign was in deep trouble after Iowa. Certainly
Kennedy helped create the expectations against which reporters evaluated his Iowa showing when he labeled the
caucuses the first "true test" of the campaign. Nonetheless, reporters concluded—on the basis of a media event
that does not produce meaningful results and a straw poll
in Florida—that Kennedy was not a viable challenger to
President Carter. In retrospect, Kennedy might have been
wiser to concede Iowa as "Carter country," noting the

state's 1976 role in making Carter the Democratic front-runner, the excellent Carter organization already in place when he entered the 1980 race, and the special feeling many Iowans held for Carter because of his previous stays in their homes and communities. That strategy might have failed as well, but the media expectations for Kennedy in Iowa might have been lower.

In the case of Ronald Reagan, the opposite was true. He had been judged the front-runner by virtually everyone who engaged in the expectations game, and his decision to remain "above" the Iowa campaign was viewed very negatively by the media. He was uniformly judged the loser in the *Des Moines Register* debate for not participating (Jones 1981, 80). It is likely, based on his 1976 showing and the fact that he carried Iowa in the general election, that if he had just "played the game," Reagan probably would have been the winner in the caucus straw poll. He did not win, however, and the media interpretation of Bush's "big" victory in Iowa created a challenger.

The Iowa precinct caucuses forced Reagan to alter his campaign strategy or face a continued negative press treatment. Reagan indicated in a Los Angeles press conference the day after the caucuses that as a result of Iowa he would campaign harder in person and would probably begin making joint appearances with other Republican candidates (Clymer 1980c, A1). With the New Hampshire primary election still five weeks away, Reagan had time to recover from the Iowa loss, and he became a very active campaigner in that state. Perhaps the final act in transforming the campaign from a passive to an active state took place when Reagan fired his campaign manager, John Sears, on the eve of the New Hampshire primary (*Newsweek* March 10, 1980, 26–34). Three months later, when addressing the Iowa Republican party's state convention, Reagan credited the later success of his campaign to the changes made as a result of the Iowa loss in January (Flansburg and Yepsen 1980a, 1A).

The 1980 precinct caucuses again demonstrated that

the winners and losers in presidential nominating contests are those who exceed or fail to meet the expectations of the unofficial handicappers. Winning by a small margin in the Republican caucus poll can be a "big" victory if unexpected, and losing by a two-to-one margin in the battle for Democratic delegates becomes a knockout blow when the magnitude of the loss exceeds expectations. The essence of the early presidential race in 1980 seems to have been expectations and perceptions, and Iowa played a major role in shaping both.

A Media Event under Fire

Efforts to limit the impact of Iowa and New Hampshire in the nominating process were renewed after the 1980 caucuses and primary elections. The Democratic National Committee (DNC) appointed the Commission on Presidential Nominations (the Hunt Commission) to consider a number of changes in the nominating process. The commission's January 15, 1982, report included a recommendation (proposed rule 10) that the length of the Democratic primary schedule be compressed into a thirteen-week period between the second Tuesday in March and the second Tuesday in June. In deference to Iowa and New Hampshire, the rule granted permanent exemptions from this time frame for the Iowa and New Hampshire nominating events, although both had to be held later in 1984. (Iowa could hold its Democratic caucuses no earlier than fifteen days before the start of the thirteen-week period; and New Hampshire, seven days.) The exception gave Iowa and New Hampshire the opportunity to focus national attention on their primary events as in the past. The recommendations were accepted by the DNC on March 26, 1982, and were made part of the rules of the national party.

Following the DNC decision, a dispute developed between New Hampshire and Vermont over the date of Vermont's Town Meeting Day, which includes a presidential straw poll and which is traditionally held on the first Tuesday in March. In 1984 that fell on March 6, which was the scheduled date for the New Hampshire presidential primary. The DNC-approved thirteen-week "window" did not apply to nonbinding electoral events such as Vermont's. The potential for conflict between the two states apparently had been underestimated by the Hunt Commission. Although the commission members were well aware of the date of the Vermont straw poll, they did not believe it necessary to schedule the New Hampshire primary election earlier than March 6. (For the DNC position on this, see Campbell et al. v. Iowa State Democratic Central Committee.) New Hampshire and the DNC were unsuccessful in resolving the conflict, and the New Hampshire Democrats, not wanting to share the limelight with Vermont on March 6, defied the national party's rules and moved its primary election forward a week to February 28.

Predictably, the decision, which would have narrowed the separation between the New Hampshire primary election and the Iowa caucuses to a single day, was not well received in Iowa. The general assembly reacted to the threat to Iowa's famous caucuses by passing legislation requiring that the precinct caucuses be held at least eight days earlier than any other nominating event (Ia. Gen. Assem. 1983, chap. 138, p. 306).

The Iowa Democratic party also reacted strongly to the threat. Fearful that the state's impact on the national nominating process would be greatly diminished, the Iowa Democrats discussed changing the date of their 1984 caucuses at a November 19, 1983, meeting of the state central committee. John Law, a former executive director of the Iowa Democratic party and a member of the Hunt Commission, informed the committee that a commission compromise had led to the new party rules governing the length of the primary and caucus schedule, and it was his understanding that Iowa had been guaranteed an eight-day separation between the New Hampshire and Iowa events. He further argued that if New Hampshire violated party rules by moving its primary election forward and the DNC did not force them back into compliance, Iowa should advance its caucus date to maintain the eight-day separation. Members of the DNC compliance committee in attendance argued against a change in caucus dates and threatened disciplinary action against the Iowa Democratic party if national party rules were violated. The debate became spirited and sometimes animated before William Sueppel of Iowa City proposed a compromise that ultimately carried by a vote of 20 to 10. The Iowa caucuses would be held on February 20, 1984, unless New Hampshire decided on or before December 10, 1983, to return its primary election to the original March 6 date. If New Hampshire relented, the Iowa caucuses would be held on February 27 as originally scheduled. The deadline passed without action by New Hampshire, and the Iowa Democrats proceeded with plans for a February 20 caucus date in 1984.

The controversy over the decision to change the caucus date did not end on December 10, however. In Iowa, three prominent Democrats—Edward Campbell, former state party chair and cochair of the Mondale for President effort in Iowa, Jean Haugland, also a Mondale cochair, and Charles Gifford, a member of the state central committee—filed suit in federal district court to block the change from February 27 to February 20. The plaintiffs requested that "the Court enjoin the State Party from holding statewide caucuses on a date prior to the 27th day of February, 1984, as an earlier date would jeopardize the seating of Iowa delegates at the Democratic National Convention" (Campbell et. al. 1984, 2). In testimony, Mr. Gifford further asserted that "the State Party is obligated to follow the clear dictates of the National Party Rules and that failure to do so may well jeopardize Iowa's first-in-the-nation status in future election years" (Campbell et al. 1984, 10).

In defending the decision to move the caucus date forward, the state party, with presidential candidates Alan Cranston and John Glenn as intervenors, argued that the campaigns of some presidential candidates would suffer irreparable harm due to their large expenditures of time and money in Iowa if the date were not changed to February 20 (Campbell et al. 1984, 13).

The court ruled in favor of the defendants and let stand the earlier date. In the decision the court agreed that the plaintiffs were entitled to relief but found for the defendants because "the intervenor presidential candidates will suffer a significant harm if the caucuses are not held on February 20, as their previous commitments may be wasted or reduced in effectiveness." The court added that "the individual damages that may be suffered by the plaintiffs are outweighed by the irreparable harm that changing the rules of the presidential nominating process [in Iowa] at this late date may have" (Campbell et al. 1984, 13).

As the plaintiffs noted, the DNC had threatened sanctions if Iowa moved its caucus date forward, including the possibility of not seating the Iowa delegation selected by the "illegal" caucus process at the Democratic National Convention. Ultimately the DNC relented, and on May 3, 1984, it agreed to seat both the Iowa and New Hampshire delegations at San Francisco.

References

Birnbaum, Irving. 1986. Telephone interview with author, July 8. Birnbaum is the owner of Omni Computers in Des Moines.

Bittick, Scott. 1980. Interview with author, January 23. Bittick was a caucus member.

Bonsignoir, Lou. 1986. Telephone interview with author, July 16. Bonsignoir was the organization director of the Iowa Republican party from 1979 to 1980.

Broder, David. 1980. "Kennedy's Challenge Suffers Big Setback." *Washington Post*, January 22, pp. A1, A4.

Bullard, Charles, and Debra Kneeland. 1980. "Ruan, Candidate Fall Short in 'Mighty 74.' " *Des Moines Register*, January 22, p. 1B.

Campbell, Edward, et al. v. Iowa State Democratic Central Committee and David Nagel. 1984. No. 83-115-W, 6 (Southern District of Iowa, January 17).

Clymer, Adam. 1980a. "Candidates and Issues: Caucus Day in Iowa." *Des Moines Register*, January 20, p. 4C.

_____. 1980b. "Carter Wins Strong Victory in Iowa as Bush Takes Lead over Reagan." *New York Times*, January 22, pp. A1, A16.

_____. 1980c. "Candidates Shifting Tactics." *New York Times*, January 23, pp. A1, A16.

Congressional Quarterly Weekly Report. 1980-83.

Democratic National Committee. 1978. Delegate Selection Rules for the 1980 Democratic National Convention. Mimeographed.

Des Moines Register. 1979-80.

Federal Election Commission. 1981. *FEC Reports on Financial Activity, 1979-1980: Final Report, Presidential Pre-Nomination Campaigns.* Washington, D.C.: Federal Election Commission.

Flansburg, James. 1979a. "Ames Dinner Attracts Eight GOP Candidates." *Des Moines Register*, October 13, p. 4A.

_____. 1979b. "Reagan: Debate Decision Based on Unity Wish." *Des Moines Register*, December 15, p. 16A.

_____. 1979c. "Iowa Forum is Virtually Ruled Out: President Cites Iran and Afghan Crises." *Des Moines Register*, December 29, pp. 1A, 5A.

_____. 1979d. "Carter Is Busy in Iran, But There's a Credibility Gap." *Des Moines Register*, December 30, p. 2C.

Flansburg, James. 1980a. "Decisive Week for Kennedy Campaign." *Des Moines Register*, January 6, pp. 1B, 3B.

_____. 1980b. "Brown Drops from Caucus Race." *Des Moines Register*, January 17, pp. 1A, 9A.

Flansburg, James, and Daniel Pedersen. 1979. "President's Slick Machine." *Des Moines Register*, October 21, pp. 1A, 5A, 6A.

Flansburg, James, Daniel Pedersen, and David Yepsen. 1979. "Dole, Crane Candidacies Seem Doomed: Speculation Arises at Dinner in Ames." *Des Moines Register*, October 15, pp. 1A, 4A.

Flansburg, James, James Risser, and Diane Graham. 1980. "Forum Backs Hostage Policy: But Blames Carter for Crisis." *Des Moines Register*, January 6, pp. 1A, 4A.

Flansburg, James, and David Yepsen. 1979. "Reagan's Iowa Drive Loses Steam." *Des Moines Register*, October 28, pp. 1A, 13A.

_____. 1980a. "Reagan: Loss in Iowa Aided My Campaign." *Des Moines Register*, June 8, pp. 1A, 4A.

_____. 1980b. "Culver Raps Effort to Bar Anderson." *Des Moines Register*, June 15, pp. 1A, 10A.

Flansburg, James, David Yepsen, and Daniel Pedersen. 1979. "GOP Hopefuls in Iowa." *Des Moines Register*, October 14, pp. 1A, 8A.

Germond, Jack, and Jules Witcover. 1979a. "Stacking Deck for Bush?" *Des Moines Register*, October 1, p. 10A.

_____. 1979b. "Reagan Slipping in Iowa, Or Just Waiting for the Kill?" *Des Moines Register*, November 12, p. 10A.

Graham, Diane. 1979. "ABC to Cover Both Debates Live from Des Moines." *Des Moines Register*, December 19, p. 4A.

Hainey, Mark. 1980. "In Media Event, Media Are Part of the Event." *Des Moines Register*, January 22, p. 5A.

Hyde, Tim. 1986. Telephone interviews with author, July 3, 17. Hyde was the executive director of the Iowa Republican party from 1980 to 1983.

Iowa. General Assembly. 1983. *Acts and Resolutions*. Des Moines: State of Iowa.

The Iowa Poll. 1980–81. Vols. for 1979 and 1980. Des Moines: Des Moines Register and Tribune Company.

Jones, Charles O. 1981. "Nominating Carter's Favorite Opponent: The Republicans in 1980." In *The American Elections of 1980*, edited by Austin Ranney, 61–98. Washington, D.C.: American Enterprise Institute.

Leavitt, Paul. 1979. "Gov. Brown Accepts Bid to D.M. Debate." *Des Moines Register*, December 4, pp. 1A, 7A.

Mitofsky, Warren. 1986. Telephone interview with author, July 9. Mitofsky is the director of the elections and survey unit of CBS News.

Newsweek. 1979–80.

New York Times. 1980.

Pedersen, Daniel. 1980. "Forum Backs Hostage Policy: They Came to Hear, Question, Decide." *Des Moines Register*, January 6, pp. 1A, 5A.

Pedersen, Daniel, James Flansburg, and David Yepsen. 1979. "Mondale Dismayed at White House Anger on Clark Defection." *Des Moines Register*, November 4, pp. 1A, 12A.

Pedersen, Daniel, and David Yepsen. 1980. "Bush Assails Reagan Plan on Welfare." *Des Moines Register*, January 21, pp. 1A, 3A.

Perry, James, and Albert Hunt. 1980. "Carter and Bush Win 1st Round but Have No Knockdowns Yet." *Wall Street Journal*, January 23, pp. 1, 37.

Peterson, Bill. 1980. "Baker Distant Third in the Iowa Caucuses." *Washington Post*, January 22, pp. A1, A5.

Plissner, Martin. 1986. Telephone interviews with author, June 18, July 7. Plissner is the executive political director of CBS Television.

Roberts, Trish. 1984. Interview with author, February 11. Roberts is a reporter for National Public Television.

Robinson, Michael J. 1981. "The Media in 1980: Was the Message the Message?" In *The American Elections of 1980*, edited by Austin Ranney, 177–211. Washington, D.C.: American Enterprise Institute.

Robinson, Michael J., and Margaret A. Sheehan. 1983. *Over the Wire and on TV: CBS and UPI in Campaign '80*. New York: Russell Sage Foundation.

Smith, Hedrick. 1980. "Reagan Defeated by Bush in Iowa; Carter Deals Kennedy Big Setback: Senator Assesses Campaign." *New York Times*, January 23, pp. A1, A17.

Sperling, Godfrey, Jr. 1980. "Carter, Bush: What Iowa Victories Mean." *Christian Science Monitor*, January 23, pp. 1, 10.

Television News Index and Abstracts. 1975–76, 1979–80. Nashville: Vanderbilt University.

Time. 1980.

Washington Post. 1980.

Yepsen, David. 1979a. "2nd District Tally Favors Bush, Connally." *Des Moines Register*, October 12, p. 6A.

———. 1979b. "Inconclusive Results Seen in Straw Poll." *Des Moines Register*, November 6, p. 3A.

———. 1986. Telephone interview with author, July 7. Yepsen is the chief political reporter for the *Des Moines Register*.

★★★★★ **7** ★★★★★★★★★★

The 1984 Caucuses:
The Kickoff of a
Front-Loaded Season

In addition to shortening the presidential primary season, the Hunt Commission proposals had the unintended consequence of contributing to the front-loading of the 1984 primary and caucus calendar. A number of states, anxious to share the influence and attention gained by Iowa and other states that hold early contests and aware that Iowa was now limited in terms of how early it might hold caucuses, moved their electoral events closer to the beginning of the nominating season. Seventeen states scheduled primary elections or caucuses in the first twenty-two days of the 1984 primary period (*CQ* Dec. 10, 1983, 2605).

Other Hunt Commission proposals accepted by the Democratic National Committee gave states greater flexibility in selecting delegates to the national convention. They could hold primary elections, caucuses, or a combination of the two. The greater flexibility and the perceived harmful effects of primary elections on state party organizations led to a resurgence of the caucus and convention system in 1984. Iowa had demonstrated that its early caucus system was an excellent party-building

Portions of this chapter were published as "Protecting Iowa's First-in-the-Nation Status: The 1984 Precinct Caucuses," in the *Annals of Iowa*. Used by permission of the Iowa State Historical Department.

mechanism, and other state parties moved in that direction. Whereas thirty-five states selected 71 percent of the delegates to the 1980 Democratic National Convention by primary election, only twenty-three states (and the District of Columbia and Puerto Rico) used primaries to select 54 percent of the 1984 delegates (Pomper 1985, 9).

Precaucus Activity

Some wondered if the Iowa precinct caucuses would be lost in the shuffle with so many states holding early caucuses and primaries in 1984. Others, like Senator John Glenn, thought the front-loading made Iowa and New Hampshire even more important, since successful candidates would get a quick start in what could be a very short race, and there would be very little time to recover from defeats in those states (Yepsen 1983a, 11A). A definitive answer as to the impact of front-loading would not be available until much later, but early signs indicated that presidential candidates were again taking the Iowa caucuses very seriously. A 1982 national magazine article began, "Believe it or not, the 1984 presidential race is already on" in Iowa. The story went on to describe visits by seven Democratic hopefuls seeking support for a nominating event still nearly two years away (*Newsweek* May 24, 1982, 31). It began to appear that the time spent by Iowa Democrats in defending their caucuses' first-in-the-nation status had been well worth the effort.

By 1984 the precinct caucuses had been institutionalized as a significant part of the primary and caucus schedule. The 1980 efforts by Carter, Kennedy, and Bush demonstrated that a strong organization was necessary to compete in the precinct caucuses now that Iowa was a well-publicized event in the presidential nominating process. It would no longer be possible for a candidate to put together an organization quietly and surprise the media, as McGovern had done in 1972 and as Carter had done to a lesser degree in 1976. To do well in Iowa would require a major organizational effort, but with New Hampshire a week later and Super Tuesday and its ten state delegate selection events only three weeks after the caucuses, candidate efforts could not be concentrated in the state, as they had been when several weeks separated Iowa and New Hampshire.

The Democratic Campaign.   Visits by Democratic presidential candidates were common in Iowa from 1982 to 1984 as they worked to enlist supporters and develop an organization capable of identifying and turning out potential caucus supporters. Most of the Democratic hopefuls made strong efforts and spent large sums of money and energy pursuing support for the caucuses, but it was no contest from the start. Minnesota native Walter Mondale was well known in Iowa. On campaign trips to the state he played on his close ties to Iowa by referring to himself as "Iowa's third senator," or when criticizing Republican senators Charles Grassley and Roger Jepsen on a visit to Drake University, as "Iowa's only senator."

Mondale opened a Des Moines campaign headquarters in early 1983, and by the end of the year there were twenty-two full-time employees and a large budget, computers, phone banks, district offices, and hundreds of volunteers. His staff's systematic approach to organization building included personally contacting 2500 party activists, canvasing all those who had attended the 1980 Democratic caucuses, and generally attempting to stimulate enthusiasm for the Mondale candidacy (Leavitt 1983, 1B, 6B). He received early support from the United Auto Workers and the Iowa State Education Association. The support of organized groups and endorsements from many prominent Iowa Democrats helped Mondale to develop an organization that was called "clearly superior to others" (*CQ* Dec. 10, 1983, 2601). Mondale took an early lead in the polls, never relinquished his front-runner status, and entered the final stages of the Iowa campaign with a commanding lead.

Front-runner status, however, is a mixed blessing. It assures high media visibility and easy access to political circles closed to lesser candidates, but it also creates very high expectations. Russell Baker satirically warned Mondale that as the expected winner, the press would evaluate his progress more critically:

Rotten luck . . . Mondale, we've made you the front-runner. . . . Without a front-runner, we'd have nobody to suffer surprising setbacks in the early stage of the campaign, and without surprising setbacks we would be stuck with a very dull story. We can't get people interested in a bunch of solemn clunks talking about complicated problems of government, Mondale. We've got to have a horse race or nobody's going to watch. It's tough, but somebody's got to make the sacrifice and be the front-runner. . . . Say you get only 47 percent of that boondocks vote (in Iowa and New Hampshire). What we'll do is say, well 47 percent may not be disgraceful, but Mondale had been expected to do better, so it looks like he's all washed up. . . . We of the press and TV do the expecting. You do the disappointing. That way we work together to give the country an entertaining story. (Baker 1983, 12)

Not surprisingly, Baker's satirical warning was an accurate prediction of things to come.

Other Democrats also made significant organizational efforts in the state, but with Mondale enjoying a seemingly insurmountable lead, they fought it out for second place and hoped for a stronger-than-predicted finish. Alan Cranston was probably the next best organized of the Democratic candidates, and the fifty-five days and $727,358 that he spent in Iowa in the two years prior to the 1984 caucuses were among the top figures for both categories. Cranston's message was "peace and jobs," and he made nuclear disarmament the central issue of his campaign. As the campaign progressed, he struggled to overcome the issue of his age and the perception that he was a single-issue candidate. Cranston was well known in Iowa by the time of the caucuses, and he hoped for a second- or third-place finish in the battle for delegates (Yepsen 1984d, 5A).

Gary Hart was one of the first candidates to open an Iowa office, but his was a campaign of fits and starts. His campaign was hindered by several problems, and it took him a long time to develop an effective organization. After the early start, Hart severely damaged his Iowa effort by moving his state coordinator and most of the Iowa staff to Wisconsin to contest a straw poll held there in June 1983. He finished a poor third in the Wisconsin poll and "sent a signal to Iowa Democrats that they weren't being taken very seriously" (Germond and Witcover 1985, 51). The Hart campaign returned after the Wisconsin debacle strapped for funds and minus its Iowa campaign director, who had resigned. With very limited financial resources, Hart adopted a new strategy dubbed the "van caravan." The owner of the van, Steve Lynch of Lawler, drove Hart from small town to small town, particularly in western Iowa. Hart gave speeches and met and talked with anyone likely to participate in or have an impact on the precinct caucuses. The van also served as a mobile press-conference room, and reporters and editors from small-town weekly newspapers were invited to interview Hart on the road. Although very taxing of the candidate's time—he spent over sixty days in Iowa—the Hart campaign was consistently front-page news in small-town Iowa (Yepsen 1984b, 1M; Germond and Witcover 1985, 130–31).

John Glenn did not have to struggle to develop name recognition in Iowa, as did most of the other presidential hopefuls; the former astronaut drew huge crowds whenever he campaigned in the state. But he had trouble attracting supporters for the caucuses (Yepsen, Healey, and Fuson 1984, 1A). The national press established Glenn as the most viable alternative to Mondale, but he apparently never understood the nature of a caucus organization because he ran a primary election race in Iowa. He did not employ his large staff—thirty-six full-time employees—and his financial resources effectively, which eventually led to staff shake-ups in both his Iowa and national organizations (Yepsen 1983b, 4B; Fuson and Healey 1984, 1M). The $759,178 spent by his campaign in Iowa included heavy expenditures on television, which may work well in a primary election but which generally produces few results in precinct caucuses. (As mentioned earlier, John Connally unsuccessfully employed the same approach in the 1980 caucuses.) It also appears that Glenn misjudged the political climate of Iowa. His "sensible center" message was not well received by likely Democratic caucus participants, who, unlike most Iowans, may lean toward the liberal side of the political spectrum (Yepsen 1984d, 5A).

Reubin Askew's forty-seven campaign days in Iowa were exceeded only by Hart and Cranston, but his attempts to organize the right wing of the party, and particularly the antiabortion vote, were not appreciated by Iowa Democrats, who had seen that group help defeat Democratic candidates in three recent Iowa general elections (Yepsen 1984c, 15A). Askew eventually ran short of money and canceled last-minute television messages.

Ernest Hollings also came to Iowa early, but after appearing in the state several times in 1982 and 1983, he decided to concentrate his efforts in New Hampshire. Apparently realizing that his chances for success in the caucuses were slim, Hollings decided to allocate his limited resources elsewhere. When Hollings did appear in Iowa in 1984 for forums and debates, he was a press favorite. Unlike those seriously contesting the caucuses, he had little to lose, and his candor and wit were diversions from the more serious campaign rhetoric of the other candidates.

Jesse Jackson tested the Iowa political climate on a quick trip in March 1983 (Germond and Witcover 1985, 68) and decided that a state that required a major organizational effort and included a minority population of less than 2 percent was no place to kick off his presidential campaign.

George McGovern entered the contest late, and although the sentimental favorite of many Iowans, he had difficulty overcoming the perception that he was not a serious candidate (Yepsen 1984d, 5A). He was a familiar sight in Iowa in the later months of the race, campaigning for thirty-seven days in the state. He never really developed a significant organization, but he appeared and performed well in debates and public forums, often playing the role of party sage. In that role he attempted to prevent party divisiveness by keeping the campaign rhetoric directed against Ronald Reagan.

Not only did the campaign begin much earlier in many states in 1984, but also a number of state parties initiated straw polls. By the time of the Iowa Jefferson-Jackson Day dinner in October, five states had already held major straw polls, and their results had been widely reported (Peterson 1983, A3). The media and the candidates took these early indicators very seriously, as shown by Hart's effort in Wisconsin and the national coverage given the results.

The Jefferson-Jackson Day dinner on October 8 was the most successful fund-raising event ever held by the Iowa Democratic party (Whitney 1986). The event, held in Veteran's Auditorium in Des Moines, drew about 6000 people and seven presidential candidates. The speakers list also was large, and eighteen speeches lasting about three hours tested the resolve of those who remained to hear Mondale, the last speaker of the evening. The order of appearance of the presidential hopefuls was determined by draw, and Mondale, having the final word, centered his attack on John Glenn. Glenn had criticized Mondale on a number of occasions as the candidate of special interests, and Mondale chose this opportunity to even the score. He took Glenn to task for a number of his stands on issues, but particularly for his support of President Reagan's 1981 tax cut. Looking directly at Glenn, Mondale thundered that that would have been a good time to stand up to the special interests. Mondale's controversial theme, "I am the only real Democrat," began to emerge during this speech.

Presumably, the thousands seated in the balcony of

Veteran's Auditorium had each paid ten dollars to witness the party spectacle and participate in the preference poll. (A total of 2600 dinner tickets at forty dollars each and 3600 balcony tickets at ten dollars were sold [Raines 1983, 33].) I do not know how typical my immediate area was, but everyone in the vicinity, including my party of eight, had received complimentary tickets from either the Mondale or Cranston campaigns. Some asserted that Cranston had more tickets than takers for his free passes (Germond and Witcover 1985, 109). The lopsided results of the Associated Press straw poll shown in Table 7.1 tend to confirm that most of the tickets were purchased by Mondale and Cranston.

Table 7.1.   1983 Jefferson-Jackson Day Poll Results

	Preferences	Percentage of total
Mondale	1948	47.0
Cranston	1534	37.0
Glenn	243	5.9
Uncommitted	149	3.6
Hart	146	3.5
McGovern	74	1.8
Askew	35	0.8
Hollings	14	0.3
	4143	99.9

Source: Data from the *Des Moines Register* Oct. 9, 1983, 1A; and Peterson 1983, A3.

The media concluded that the Jefferson-Jackson Day fund-raiser was so obviously stacked by Mondale and Cranston that they discounted the results of the now-famous preference poll. The outcome was widely reported, but most stories downplayed the poll's significance. The *New York Times* reported the results but thought that "by using the straw poll mainly to raise money, the state Democratic Party undermined its legitimacy" (Raines 1983, 33). *Time* magazine's story on the dinner did not mention the poll (Oct. 24, 1983, 28, 29). The irony of the 1983 preference poll is that Mondale and Cranston were too successful in packing the hall. Carter used the same tactic in 1975, but with much less success. Consequently, Carter's more modest victory was widely interpreted as a significant win, while Mondale and Cranston gained little for outdistancing the field in 1983.

Concurrent with the reporting of the Jefferson-Jackson Day poll, and in many cases in the same story, the results of an October Iowa Poll were reported to the nation. That poll, like national Gallup samplings, found the Democratic contest to be a two-person race between Walter Mondale and John Glenn, with those who reported that they "definitely or probably" would attend a precinct caucus divided as follows: Mondale, 46 percent; Glenn, 27; Hart, 7; McGovern, 5; Jackson, 2; Cranston, Askew, and Hollings, 1 percent or less; and 10 percent were undecided (*Iowa Poll: 1983*, poll no. 1109).

The national media seemed to rely heavily on national and state public opinion polls in developing the two-candidate-race scenario. Critics argued that polls of the general public tend to reflect levels of name recognition, not organized political support, which is so crucial in the early nominating events (*Newsweek* Dec. 12, 1983, 72). The research presented here documents that the Iowa Poll had been a *very poor* indicator of candidate standing prior to earlier Iowa caucuses, and 1984 would again demonstrate the folly of developing precaucus expectations on the basis of public opinion polls, even when the respondents assure pollsters that they plan to attend the meetings.

Where the 1980 caucus campaign was characterized by dinners and events that conducted preference polls, the 1984 race featured candidate debates and forums. The *Des Moines Register* announced on May 14 that it would sponsor a precaucus debate for Democratic presidential candidates nine months later, on February 11, 1984, at the Des Moines Civic Center. In the months following the *Regis-*

ter's announcement, several other organizations scheduled presidential forums, each of which drew several candidates and the media.

On August 13, 1983, a committee known as People Encouraging Arms Control Efforts (PEACE) organized an "Open Forum on Arms Control with the Presidential Candidates" in Des Moines. Five of the six announced Democratic presidential hopefuls—Cranston, Glenn, Hart, Hollings, and Mondale—completed a questionnaire developed by STAR*PAC (Stop the Arms Race Political Action Committee of Iowa) and agreed to appear at the nuclear-arms forum. The only candidate not accepting the invitation, Reubin Askew, did not want to be associated with the nuclear freeze movement. (Hollings canceled at the last moment due to the death of his infant granddaughter.) The all-day affair included workshops and a three-hour question-and-answer session for the presidential candidates moderated by one of its prime movers, Iowa congressman Berkley Bedell. The forum attracted a large audience of about 1800 to 2000 people and national press and television coverage.

The forum was something of a landmark for nuclear freeze groups in Iowa, since it gave the movement legitimacy. A sitting congressman and five presidential candidates were willing to come together and openly compete for the support of Iowa peace groups. The audience was, for the most part, young and liberal, but it also included large numbers of older middle-class people. It appeared that the young activists of an earlier day were now older and still very opposed to the use of nuclear arms. Senator Cranston, the most outspoken foe of nuclear weapons of the forum participants, attempted to build his campaign in Iowa around the issue.

The ground rules prevented the Democratic participants from criticizing each other, and although they spent time attacking President Reagan's arms control and nuclear policies, the *New York Times* thought the forum "drew out some of the differences, some subtle and some

not, between the four candidates who participated" (Gailey
1983, A17). Other columnists were even more enthusiastic
about the peace forum. A story by Germond and Witcover
called the forum "the single most revealing exercise in the
eight months of the campaign for the Democratic presidential nomination" (1983, 8A).

A second forum, sponsored by the Black-Brown Coali-
tion in Des Moines on January 10, 1984, centered on civil
rights issues, particularly minority representation in government. Four presidential hopefuls—Cranston, Glenn,
Hart, and McGovern—attended, and they agreed on most
issues. A panel of minority-community activists questioned the candidates and pressed for specific plans, particularly plans for increasing minority representation in the
federal bureaucracy and judiciary. The four assailed Mondale for his absence and called for increased spending for
educational programs and a greater role for blacks and Hispanics in government. One of the few areas of disagreement came over government efforts to limit immigration.
Glenn favored, and the other three opposed, identification
cards for Hispanics (Yepsen, Fuson, and Healey 1984, 1M,
6M).

A third forum, on farm issues, was held in Ames on
January 21. Six candidates—Askew, Cranston, Hart, Hollings, McGovern, and Mondale—appeared before a crowd of
approximately 1500 people on the Iowa State University
campus. Cranston took the only unpopular stand of the
day when he proclaimed that the parity index was outdat-
ed as a basis for grain prices. The statement drew boos and
one man in the audience stood and proclaimed, "Boy, are
you dumb!" The remaining hopefuls, minus Glenn, who
was absent because of a previous commitment in the
South, played it safe and attempted to blame all of the ills
of the farm economy on President Reagan (Yepsen 1984a,
3A).

The grand finale of the forum season was the *Des
Moines Register*'s debate on February 11 in Des Moines.
The *Register* spent months planning and promoting the

Where the 1980 caucus campaign was characterized by dinners and events at which preference polls were conducted, the 1984 Democratic race featured candidate debates and forums. The grand finale of the forum season was a debate sponsored by the *Des Moines Register*, which featured eight presidential candidates. The event attracted an audience of approximately 2500 people and about 200 reporters.

event, even holding a drawing for the approximately 2500 tickets available to the general public. Eight presidential candidates—Askew, Cranston, Glenn, Hart, Hollings, Jackson, McGovern, and Mondale—participated in the forum, the format of which permitted two-minute opening statements, followed by three rounds of the candidates questioning each other, followed by another round of questions from six panelists, and concluding with a two-minute closing statement by each.

The forum was a media spectacular covered by about 200 reporters representing "every major newspaper, all the networks," and local and regional broadcast systems. CNN provided live television coverage, and the Public Broadcasting Service and C-Span taped and broadcast the event on a delayed basis. Additional live coverage was provided by radio stations throughout the state (Yepsen and Healey 1984, 1A, 11A).

The forum was a time for the candidates to reiterate familiar themes. With the campaign almost two years old, their positions were well developed and were well known to the active Democrats most likely to attend the precinct caucuses. Most seemed to be trying to avoid mistakes before the largest audience of the campaign, but there were notable exceptions. Hollings and Jackson delighted the crowd with their candor and glibness, and McGovern made an impassioned plea to his supporters, asking them not to "throw away your conscience" by supporting a different candidate simply because it was widely believed that he, McGovern, had little chance in 1984. "Reagan bashing" was the most popular activity of the forum as candidate after candidate attacked the "failed" policies of the administration.

The two and a half hours passed rather quickly, and those in attendance seemed to enjoy being part of the *Register*'s forum. It is debatable, however, whether such events have an impact on the caucus process. Perhaps they serve to stimulate interest, which could increase attendance and have an impact on some meetings, but it is unlikely that they alter support patterns significantly.

The media, with their "game" focus, concentrated their efforts on determining who had won or lost the debate. In the four days following the forum, the *Des Moines Register* analyzed the performance of each of the participants and conducted a statewide poll asking respondents which of the candidates impressed them favorably or unfavorably in the debate. The newspaper concluded that McGovern had won the debate on the basis of a 40%–4% favorable–unfavorable rating among likely caucus participants. Mondale, who apparently just met the writer's expectations, "didn't lose ground" with his 47%–11% ranking, but Glenn (16%–13%) and Hollings (7%–13%) "were the only candidates who made about as many bad impressions as good" and were judged the losers (Ebert 1984, 1A, 13A; *Iowa Poll: 1984*, poll no. 1136).

The Republican Campaign. President Reagan was seeking reelection in 1984 and without a challenger in Iowa there was no Republican campaign. The president did not visit the state prior to the caucuses, and his absence caused at least one negative side effect. The Democratic campaign was identifying supporters and potential campaign workers for the general election struggle, and with no campaign to stimulate interest, the Republicans were unable to match the effort.

The 1984 Precinct Caucuses

The Iowa campaign came to an end, and the soft evidence provided by the polls, debates, and political pundits had been analyzed and re-analyzed. The candidates had made extraordinary efforts in Iowa, and their campaign activity is summarized in Table 7.2. Democratic

Table 7.2.   1984 Candidate Precaucus Campaign Activity and
            Spending

	Days in Iowa	Spending in Iowa
Askew	47	$194,315
Cranston	55	727,358
Glenn	33	759,178
Hart	60	453,503
Hollings	14	11,382
Jackson	2	8,953
McGovern	37	52,403
Mondale	34	687,712
Reagan	1	194,821

Source: Spending data are from the Federal Election Commission report *FEC Reports on Financial Activity, 1983–84: Final Report, Presidential Pre-Nomination Campaigns*, Table A9. The Iowa limit was
$684,537. The campaign activity includes 1982, 1983, and 1984. The
1982 data are from the *Iowa Democratic Party Data Book: 1983–84*. The
1983 and 1984 data were collected from the individual campaigns and
are of varying reliability. Most of the campaigns provided sound information that included dates and cities visited. The Hart and Mondale campaigns provided information of lesser quality. The Hart people, for example, reported that he was in Iowa only five times in 1984 and on
twenty-seven occasions during the three-year period. Our examination of
the *Des Moines Register* indicated that Hart was in the state at least sixty
days.

presidential candidates spent about 300 days in the state,
building organizations and engaging in the personal style
of campaigning that Iowans have come to expect. Federal
financial reports show that Glenn, Cranston, and Mondale
reached the federal limit on campaign spending in Iowa,
and Hart was not far behind. Again, federal reports probably understate campaign expenditures. Mondale, for example, had strong labor support, and the unions' "independent expenditures" included phone banks operated by
labor volunteers and nineteen local headquarters rented
from unions for nominal monthly fees. Also, the rental cars
used by the Mondale campaign bore Minnesota license
plates. Glenn had a phone bank in St. Louis making Iowa
calls, and Cranston stayed in Omaha when campaigning in
western Iowa (Yepsen 1984c, 15A). It is evident from the
amount of campaign activity in the state that the compressed and front-loaded primary schedule did not

minimize the importance of the Iowa caucuses. If anything, the candidates emphasized the caucuses more than in 1980.

Media Coverage.　The media also came to Iowa very early to follow the Democratic candidates. Media coverage waxed and waned between 1982 and 1984, but on special occasions, such as the "Open Forum on Arms Control with the Presidential Candidates" in Des Moines on August 13 and the *Des Moines Register*'s debate on February 11, which was attended by all eight Democratic presidential candidates, national media attention focused on Iowa.

In the final days of the caucus campaign, reporters seeking stories searched for "typical Iowans" (those wearing bib overalls were in particular demand), and most of all played the expectations game. Mondale was judged the "clear front-runner" and John Glenn the "primary challenger" even though an effective Glenn campaign organization never developed in Iowa and his campaign showed many signs of weakness. McGovern, Hart, and Cranston made up the second tier. Hollings, Askew, and Jesse Jackson, who did not participate in the caucus race, were given little chance of success.

Media coverage for the caucuses was awesome. The press "filing space" for 1984 was double that of 1980. Over a thousand press credentials were issued by the Iowa Democratic party to representatives and technicians of approximately 150 U.S. and foreign news organizations. More than thirty television and many radio stations were represented in Iowa; "Meet the Press" and "Face the Nation" originated from Des Moines on the day before the caucuses; and on February 20, the day of the caucuses, the "Today" show and the evening news programs of ABC, CBS, NBC, and CNN originated live from Des Moines (Piatt 1984). In terms of the breadth of coverage, 1984 far exceeded 1980. If input (stories produced) is any indication of output (stories aired or printed), there were probably far more stories aired and printed about the Iowa caucuses at the international and local levels in 1984 than ever before. This was not, however, the case with the CBS television news.

Table 7.3. 1980 and 1984 CBS News Stories on Iowa and New Hampshire

	July 1, 1979–June 30, 1980			July 1, 1983–June 30, 1984		
	Weekday	Weekend	Total	Weekday	Weekend	Total
Iowa	37	17	54	8	3	11
N.H.	29	11	40	14	8	22

Source: Data were collected from the *Television News Index and Abstracts*, produced by Vanderbilt University. The criteria for constructing the table are discussed in the source note for Table 6.2.

Table 7.3 compares television coverage of the 1980 and 1984 Iowa precinct caucuses and the New Hampshire primary election by CBS's evening and weekend news for one-year periods from July 1, 1979, to June 30, 1980, and from July 1, 1983, to June 30, 1984. The data indicate that there was an overall decline in the number of Iowa and New Hampshire stories aired by CBS in 1984 compared with 1980 and that in 1984 New Hampshire was again the leading early nominations story, after relinquishing that position to Iowa in 1980. A definitive explanation is not possible, but a lengthy discussion with Martin Plissner of CBS produced some tentative thoughts about the reduced coverage (June 18, 1986). In 1980 both parties featured vigorous presidential nominating contests, while in 1984 only the Democrats had a contest. Simply stated, there was more to cover in 1980. The relatively greater decline in Iowa coverage in 1984 is less easily explained. It is possible that the compressed 1984 schedule had some impact, since Iowa was moved closer to the pack. Iowa was five weeks earlier than New Hampshire in 1980 but only eight days in 1984. Perhaps the fact that Mondale was the overwhelming favorite in the Iowa caucuses diminished media interest. Perhaps New Hampshire received greater coverage because of Hart's perceived success in Iowa.

Turnout for the 1984 precinct caucuses also suffered from lack of interest. Pollsters and party officials predicted a month before the meetings that turnout was likely to be much less than in 1980 (*DMR* Jan. 22, 1984, 2C). Democratic party officials estimated that 75,000 people attended their meetings (approximately 14 percent of the registered Democrats). Again, a definitive explanation is not possible, but Mondale's big early lead and a resulting boredom factor probably contributed to the 25 percent decline in attendance from 1980 (Steffen 1984).

The Democratic Caucuses.   In spite of their extensive coverage of the Iowa caucuses, the media had grown wary of the "results" provided by the Iowa political parties. It is well documented that the complex tabulation process confuses many reporters; the *Des Moines Register*, CBS, and other news organizations were aware that the reporting of caucus outcomes was not governed by law and had been manipulated. CBS was very concerned about the validity of caucus results because of its experiences in Iowa in 1976 and 1980 (Plissner July 7, 1986).

These concerns led news organizations to ask the Iowa Democratic party to provide a breakdown of the candidate preference of those attending the 1984 meetings after the first division into preference groups. In essence, they were asking the party to conduct a straw poll of caucus members and to provide raw vote totals rather than the delegate equivalents reported since 1972. The Iowa Democrats asserted that raw vote totals would misrepresent the caucus process and refused to bow to media demands (*DMR* Oct. 16, 1983, 2C). The media responded to the deadlock by employing the News Election Service (NES), a vote-counting service funded by ABC, CBS, NBC, AP, and UPI, to determine candidate preference totals after the first division into preference groups at the Democratic caucuses. Since the caucus process does not lend itself to tabulating candidate preference, and since the Iowa Democratic party refused to cooperate, the NES was able to provide preference totals for only 74 percent of the 2495 precincts, and its numbers were of questionable validity due to the dynamic nature of the precinct meetings. Moreover, since the NES did not weight the totals on the basis of county size, the "one man, one vote" principle was badly violated. The presence of two sets of results proved confusing to all.

After months under the media microscope and to the relief of many Iowans, the 8 P.M. time for the February 20 precinct caucuses finally arrived. But it took only twelve minutes for another controversy to erupt. On the basis of a review of sign-in sheets at some caucuses, CBS projected Walter Mondale the Iowa winner at 8:12 P.M. (CST), eighteen minutes before Democratic party rules permitted the delegate selection process to begin (U.S. Congress, House 1984, 12). NBC used polls and NES data to project at 8:18 P.M. that Mondale would be the winner, that John Glenn would not finish second, and that there was a "very good chance" that Gary Hart would be second. ABC withheld its projection that Mondale would win and that Glenn, Hart, and Cranston were "fighting it out for second place" until 8:46 P.M., sixteen minutes after the caucuses began but before any delegate counts were available (U.S. Congress, House 1984, 14).

The Iowa Democrats were very disturbed by the early media projections, and so was Congress. On February 27, 1984, the House Subcommittee on Telecommunications, Consumer Protection, and Finance held a hearing on early election projections, and it centered on the Iowa caucuses. Chairman Tim Wirth, a Democrat from Colorado, informed those present that the hearing was being held "to discuss the civic responsibility of the electronic media and the implications that their methods and their announcements of projected results have on the electoral process" (U.S. Congress, House 1984, 5). The subcommittee received a number of research papers and heard testimony from top media executives and leaders of the Republican and Democratic parties. David Nagle, the Iowa Democratic chair, testified that the state party had evidence that the early projections had found their way into caucuses that were in progress. Nagle warned that "to report the supposed outcome of our process before it even begins . . . runs the risk of seriously intruding on the process and damaging the party" (U.S. Congress, House 1984, 78).

The subcommittee continued its hearings, and late in the year two congressmen—Al Swift, a Democrat from Washington, and William M. Thomas, a Republican from California—formally asked ABC, CBS, and NBC for "a firm, explicit, public, corporate commitment not to use exit poll data to suggest, through interpretation of that data, the probable winner in any state until the polls in that state have closed" (Swift and Thomas 1984).

By early 1985 the three networks had forwarded letters to Congressmen Swift and Thomas which stated that in future elections they would not "use exit polling data to project or characterize election results until the polls are closed in [that] state" (Swift and Thomas 1985). In return, the congressmen agreed to begin hearings on uniform hours for voting on election day throughout the United States. It is not clear how the agreement will affect the reporting of Iowa caucus outcomes, but changes will likely be minimal. Perhaps the networks will follow ABC's 1984 example and not project caucus results until after the meetings begin the delegate selection process, though that would still mean that winners and losers will probably be projected while the meetings are in progress.

As caucus results began to come in on February 20, the expectations game continued, with the media interpretating the outcomes. The *Des Moines Register*, the *New York Times*, the *Wall Street Journal*, the *Christian Science Monitor*, and *Newsweek* reported NES results; the *Washington Post*, the *St. Louis Globe-Dispatch*, *U.S. News and World Report*, and *Time* carried the Democratic party's state delegate equivalent figures, and *Congressional Quarterly* reported both. The two sets of numbers are shown in Table 7.4. The official Democratic results showed Mondale, Hart, and uncommitted percentages as greater than indicated by the NES outcomes, and the others as less.

Table 7.4.   1984 Democratic Precinct Caucus Results

	State delegate equivalents (%)	News Election Service poll results (%)
Mondale	48.9	44.5
Hart	16.5	14.8
McGovern	10.3	12.6
Uncommitted	9.4	7.5
Cranston	7.4	9.0
Glenn	3.5	5.3
Askew	2.5	3.3
Jackson	1.5	2.7
Hollings	0.0	0.3

Source: The "state delegate equivalents" are the official results of the Iowa Democratic party and are based on reports from 94 percent of the precincts. The News Election Service results are from 74 percent of the precincts.

The *Newsweek* summary of the Iowa caucuses was representative. It concluded that "Mondale's victory met all expectations," and Glenn's "humiliating fifth-place finish" was a disaster for his campaign. McGovern's third-place finish was "startling," and "the caucuses gave Hart media momentum." Cranston, Askew, and Hollings were declared the big losers along with Glenn. On the basis of the Iowa caucuses, *Newsweek* reduced the field to Mondale, Hart, Jackson, "and maybe Glenn" (March 5, 1984, 22–23).

Mondale was the overwhelming winner in the caucuses, and the press headlines reflected the magnitude of his win. The *Des Moines Register* said that "Mondale Scores Easy Victory" (Feb. 21), the *New York Times* reported "Mondale Wins Handily in Iowa" (Feb. 21), and the

Washington Post headline reported that the "Winner in Iowa Ran Far Ahead of Field" (Feb. 22). The Mondale performance not only met press expectations, it exceeded them to the point that the *Christian Science Monitor* thought that Mondale had "moved so far ahead of his seven opponents that he could lock up his party's presidential nomination by mid-March" (Feb. 22, 1).

The big loser in the Iowa caucuses was John Glenn. All of the country's major newspapers emphasized how devastating the results were for his campaign. The *Des Moines Register* reported that Glenn had "faltered badly" (Feb. 21, 1A); the *New York Times* thought that the Iowa defeat "threatened to cripple his presidential candidacy" (Feb. 21, A1); the *Wall Street Journal* called the Glenn finish a "stunning defeat" (Feb. 21, 62); the *Christian Science Monitor* thought that Glenn's campaign was in "deep, deep trouble" (Feb. 22, 1); and the *Washington Post* declared that Glenn had "crash-landed" in Iowa (Feb. 22, A1).

Unlike the *Christian Science Monitor*, most newspapers and magazines were not ready to concede the nomination to Mondale, and having declared Glenn all but dead, they elevated Hart to the position of main challenger on the basis of his second-place finish in Iowa. The reporting was cautious, because Hart had finished a very distant second in the precinct caucuses, but the *Washington Post* thought that Mondale faced "a new challenge from a strengthened Sen. Gary Hart" (Feb. 22, 1A).

The new reality of the Democratic presidential contest was perhaps best outlined by Germond and Witcover in a story analyzing the impact of Iowa entitled "Iowa Caucuses Change the Candidates' Political-Expectations Game." They opined that "John Glenn has been effectively eliminated as a serious contender to Walter Mondale" because "the political community and press fully expected him to finish second, however distantly. . . . Similarly, Gary Hart has been transformed into the sole remaining serious competitor to Mondale, not because he finished

Ronald Reagan was formerly a sports reporter for WHO radio in Des Moines. As the unchallenged Republican incumbent in 1984, he was able to watch the Democrats fight it out in Iowa.

second—after all, he ran far behind Mondale—but because he showed so much more strength than the evidence suggested was reasonable to expect" (*DMR* Feb 22, 8A). It did not take long for Hart to benefit from the perception that he was the last hope to make 1984 a horse race. On the "NBC Nightly News" on February 23, Don Oliver reported that after Iowa, contributions to the Hart campaign had increased from $2,000 a day to $12,000.

The Republican Caucuses.   The Republicans also held precinct caucuses in 1984, but with an incumbent president, there was little campaigning and no media interest in their meetings until President Reagan decided to visit Iowa on February 20, the day of the caucuses. The president appeared in Waterloo and Des Moines in an attempt to increase interest in the Republican caucuses and to steal some of the limelight from the Democrats, who had monopolized media attention in Iowa for several months.

The straw poll initiated in 1976 and continued in 1980 was not conducted in the 1984 Republican caucuses. Republican officials did not think a poll necessary, since the nomination was uncontested. The absence of a poll also assured that if any dissatisfied Republicans attended the caucuses, they would not embarrass President Reagan. Attendance figures for the Republican caucuses could only be very tentative due to the absence of a poll, but it was estimated that 25,000 to 30,000 people participated (Roth 1984).

The Impact of the
1984 Caucuses

Iowans appear to have grown blasé in 1984 about their now-famous media event. The notoriety associated with the caucuses failed to stimulate the interest in and attendance at the 1984 meetings as that it had in 1980. On the other hand, Iowa's political parties and the Des Moines Chamber of Commerce were anything but blasé. The Chamber created a caucus information center in the Des Moines skywalk and promoted the media event. Friendly hostesses provided information on anything a visitor or reporter could possibly wish to know about the state and its people. The political parties increased their public relations efforts and were more helpful than ever to the press. The Democrats published a 211-page *Iowa Democratic Party Data Book*, which included everything from previous caucus results and explanations of the process to lists of hotels and motels in counties throughout the state. Everyone worked very hard to accommodate reporters and promote Iowa as a great place to begin the presidential race.

Concerns that the Iowa caucuses might be lost in the shuffle of a front-loaded nomination season proved to be unfounded. In most respects, except possibly the number of television stories aired by CBS, Iowa was a bigger media event than before. Candidate visits to the state were so numerous as to be commonplace. The volume of media coverage and the number of reporters spending time in Iowa also increased substantially. CNN became the fourth national network to set up temporary studios in Des Moines, international reporters were more in evidence, and local broadcast and press people, particularly from the major metropolitan areas, were far more evident than in past caucus seasons.

The compressed primary and caucus schedule maximized the impact of the Iowa caucuses as John Glenn had predicted. Candidates who fared poorly in the Iowa perceptions game had only eight days to recover before the primary election in New Hampshire, and the task proved too great for most. Alan Cranston, who had spent parts of two years and three-quarters of a million dollars in Iowa, announced on February 29, nine days after the Iowa caucuses and one day after the New Hampshire primary election, that he was no longer a candidate for the presidency. Hollings and Askew withdrew from the race on March 2, McGovern on March 13, and Glenn on March 16. It was indeed a very fast and short race for the majority of candidates in 1984.

But Iowa has gained its reputation as an early indicator in the presidential race not only by exposing weakness. The precinct caucuses produce "surprise winners"—candidates who do better than expected and as a result gain media momentum. There were few surprises in 1984, other than Glenn's very poor finish. Mondale met media expectations in the caucuses, but with the Glenn candidacy written off by reporters, there was a need for a challenger, and here Hart filled the bill. McGovern was something of a surprise, finishing ahead of the remainder of the second tier, but the media remembered him as the big loser to Nixon in 1972 and thus were unwilling to make too much of his relatively high finish. Hart was a new face, and although he claimed only 16.5 percent of the state delegate equivalents in Iowa, this was enough of a surprise to gain media attention. Hart was still very much a dark horse, but in the eyes of the media he was the only other horse in the race.

The new role brought Hart the media attention he had lacked before Iowa, and when he arrived in New Hampshire he found a "swollen pack of journalists" willing to trail him everywhere and report his every utterance (*Time* March 5, 1984, 8). Hart and, to a lesser extent, Mondale were the only candididates who benefited from Iowa, and with only eight days separating Iowa and New Hampshire there was no time for the others to recover. Hart went on to win in New Hampshire and in Maine six days later, and for a time at least, he was elevated to the position of front-runner. These successes were made possible by the positive media interpretation of Hart's placing a distant second in the Iowa precinct caucuses.

The Second Defense of a Media Event

Although it has cooperated with its Democratic counterpart, the Iowa Republican party has played a more limited role in defending Iowa's position of prominence. The national Republican party has no rules governing the length of the primary and caucus season, and when Iowa raised the issue at the 1984 Republican National Convention, there was little interest in developing such rules (Paulin 1984). Before 1984 there were no significant threats from other state Republican parties, and in 1984 a change in the Michigan caucus and convention system went largely unnoticed due to the lack of a contest for the Republican presidential nomination. But Michigan had moved its caucus and convention process forward, and the first step in the selection of its 1988 delegates took place on August 5, 1986, when candidates for precinct delegates were selected in the primary election. The move brought presidential hopefuls to the state and attracted some media attention.

Shortly after the 1984 Democratic National Convention, the now-predictable assault on the date of the Iowa caucuses began anew, but this time from another source. Representative Morris Udall and Senator Dennis DeConcini, both Arizona Democrats, introduced companion bills (H.R. 6054 and S. 2890) to Congress on July 31, 1984. The bills would have required that "Presidential primaries or caucuses be held only during the period beginning on the second Tuesday in March and ending on the second Tuesday in June of the year of the Presidential election." The

Task Force on Elections, which had been created by the Committee on House Administration, held a hearing on September 19, 1984, but the bills died in the Ninety-eighth Congress.

Congressman Udall reintroduced identical legislation (H.R. 1380) in the first session of the Ninety-ninth Congress on February 28, 1985. In describing the bill for the House, Udall explained that "it would make two small, but important changes in the way we choose our Presidential nominees. First, the primary season would be limited to a specific period of time, eliminating the disproportionate influence of a few early primary states. Second, a shorter primary season would reduce the amount of campaign spending and relieve some of the 'boredom factor' experienced by many voters" (*Congressional Record* Feb. 28, 1984, E 723).

If judged from a historical perspective, the likelihood of Congressman Udall successfully removing the status of Iowa and New Hampshire as major nominating events is not good; since 1911, none of the approximately 300 bills designed to reform or alter the presidential nominating process has passed Congress (Hyde 1984, 5A).

The national Democratic party did not change the order or length of the 1988 primary season, but it appears likely that Iowa will continually have to redefend its first-in-the-nation status in the presidential campaign. Without an incumbent presidential candidate in 1988, both the Republican and Democratic party races will be spirited events. The stakes are so high that in all likelihood other state parties will be tempted to follow the Michigan lead and take aim at the early date of the Iowa caucuses.

References

Baker, Russell. 1983. "Handicappers." *New York Times Magazine*, February 6, p. 12. Copyright © 1983 by The New York Times Company. Reprinted by permission.

Broder, David, and Dan Balz. 1984. "Hart Declares Contest Will Narrow to Two." *Washington Post*, February 22, pp. A1, A12.

Congressional Quarterly Weekly Report. 1983–84.

Congressional Record. 1985.

Des Moines Register. 1983–84.

Dillin, John. 1984. "Iowa Caucuses Reshuffle Field of Democrats." *Christian Science Monitor*, February 22, pp. 1, 28.

Ebert, David. 1984. "Poll Finds McGovern 'Won' Debate." *Des Moines Register*, February 17, pp. 1A, 13A.

Federal Election Commission. 1986. *FEC Reports on Financial Activity, 1983–84: Final Report, Presidential Pre-Nomination Campaigns*. Washington, D.C.: Federal Election Commission.

Fuson, Ken, and James Healey. 1984. "Glenn Replaces National Campaign Director." *Des Moines Register*, January 27, p. 1M.

Gailey, Phil. 1983. "Arms Curb Debate Sets Glenn Apart from Rivals." *New York Times*, August 16, p. A17.

Germond, Jack, and Jules Witcover. 1983. "Peace Forum a Campaign High Spot." *Des Moines Register*, August 17, p. 8A.

———. 1984. "Iowa Caucuses Change the Candidates' Political-Expectations Game. . . ." *Des Moines Register*, February 22, p. 8A.

———. 1985. *Wake Us when It's Over*. New York: Macmillan.

———. 1986. "Michigan: Early with Sound and Fury." *Des Moines Register*, June 18.

Hyde, John. 1984. "Bill Would Abolish Early Iowa Caucuses." *Des Moines Register*, September 20, p. 5A.

Iowa Democratic Party Data Book: 1983–84. 1984. Des Moines: Iowa Democratic Party.

The Iowa Poll. 1984–87. Vols. for 1983 through 1986. Des Moines Register and Tribune Company.

Leavitt, Paul. 1983. "His Business Is Selling a Political Candidate." *Des Moines Register*, December 4, pp. 1B, 6B.

———. 1984. "Iowa GOP United behind Reagan, Debates Party Issues." *Des Moines Register*, February 21, p. 1M.

Newsweek. 1982–84.

Patterson, Thomas E. 1980. *The Mass Media Election: How Americans Choose Their President*. New York: Praeger.

Paulin, Tamara. 1984. Telephone interview with author, May 7. Paulin was the organizational director of the Iowa Republican party from 1983 to 1985.

Peterson, Bill. 1983. "Iowa Polls Indicate That Mondale Is Still the Democrat to Beat." *Washington Post*, October 9, p. A3.

Peterson, Bill, and Kathy Sawyer. 1984. "Winner in Iowa Ran Far Ahead of Field." *Washington Post*, February 22, pp. A1, A8.

Piatt, Barry. 1984. Telephone interview with author, March 19. Piatt was the press secretary of the Iowa Democratic party from 1983 to 1985.

Plissner, Martin. 1983. "How Iowa's Caucuses Became the First Test." *Des Moines Register*, October 23, pp. 1C, 3C.

_____. 1986. Telephone interviews with author, June 18, July 7. Plissner is the executive political director of CBS Television.

Pomper, Gerald. 1985. "The Nominations." In *The Election of 1984: Reports and Interpretations*, edited by Gerald Pomper, 1–34. Chatham, N.J.: Chatham House.

Raines, Howell. 1983. "7 Democrats Visit a Dinner in Iowa." *New York Times*, October 9, p. 33.

_____. 1984. "Mondale Wins Handily in Iowa; Tight Race for 2nd as Glenn Trails." *New York Times*, February 21, pp. A1, A20.

Roth, Luke. 1984. Telephone interview with author, December 7. Roth was the executive director of the Iowa Republican party from 1983 to 1985.

St. Louis Globe-Dispatch. 1984.

Steffen, J. P. 1984. Interview with author, December 4. Steffen has been the caucus chair of the Iowa Democratic party since 1983.

Swift, Al, and William M. Thomas. 1984. Letter to ABC, CBS, and NBC, December 6. Washington, D.C.: U.S. House of Representatives.

_____. 1985. Press Conference, Rayburn Office Building, Washington, D.C., January 17.

Television News Index and Abstracts. 1979–80, 1983–84. Nashville: Vanderbilt University.

Time. 1983–84.

U.S. Congress. House. 1984. *Early Election Projection: The Iowa Experience*. Hearing before the Subcommittee on Telecommunications, Consumer Protection, and Finance of the Committee on Energy and Commerce, February 27. 98th Cong., 2d sess.

U.S. News and World Report. 1984.

Wall Street Journal. 1984.

Whitney, Tom. 1986. Letter to author, June 5. Whitney was the chair of the Iowa Democratic party from 1973 to 1977.

Yepsen, David. 1983a. "Off to the Races." *Des Moines Register*, May 30, p. 11A.

_____. 1983b. "Glenn's New Iowa Director Paints Rosy Picture." *Des Moines Register*, December 4, pp. 4B, 5B.

_____. 1984a. "Hart, McGovern Receive Top Marks at Farm Forum." *Des Moines Register*, January 23, p. 3A.

_____. 1984b. "Hart Turns On the Heat, Revives His Campaign in Iowa." *Des Moines Register*, January 26, p. 1M.

_____. 1984c. "Slipping Past Campaign Spending Limits in Iowa with a Little Help from Outside." *Des Moines Register*, February 6, p. 15A.

_____. 1984d. "Caucus Story May Not Be Finished until Fall." *Des Moines Register*, February 19, p. 5A.

Yepsen, David, Ken Fuson, and James R. Healey. 1984. "Four Democrats Flail Reagan over His Rights Record." *Des Moines Register*, January 11, pp. 1M, 6M.

Yepsen, David, and James R. Healey. 1984. "Democratic Rivals to Debate Today at D.M. Civic Center." *Des Moines Register*, February 11, pp. 1A, 11A.

Yepsen, David, James R. Healey, and Ken Fuson. 1984. "Leaders: Glenn May Be Red-Faced Caucus Night." *Des Moines Register*, February 5, pp. 1A, 5A.

8

Media Event or Local Event: The Iowa Precinct Caucuses in Perspective

Officials of both state parties, correspondents for the national media, and candidates for the presidency have all cooperated in making the Iowa precinct caucuses a weather vane for the presidential nominating process. The 1972 decision by the Iowa Democratic party to move its caucus date forward to implement a number of party reforms had an immediate impact on the presidential nominating process. The earlier date made Iowa the first Democratic nominating event to begin selecting delegates to the national convention, and Iowa's new first-in-the-nation status was immediately noticed by reporters and presidential candidates. Further changes in state caucus procedures by the Democrats in 1972 and 1976 and by the Republicans in 1976 and 1980 made possible the creation of a media event by instituting a common date for the meetings and providing "results" or "outcomes" from the process.

The news media, faced with the problem of covering a number of candidates in the initial stages of presidential campaigns, recognized Iowa as a source of early evidence about the progress of the race. The news trendsetters—the *New York Times* and the *Washington Post*—were among those who "discovered" the precinct caucuses, and they pointed the way to Iowa in 1976 for political reporters embarrassed by their errors of judgment in the 1972 Muskie-

McGovern race. One reporter, R. W. Apple of the *New York Times*, probably deserves the title of Father of the Iowa Media Event for focusing media attention on the local meetings. His stories about the 1972 outcomes and the surprisingly strong McGovern finish, and his stories about the 1976 Jefferson-Jackson Day preference poll, in which he alerted the nation to the strong Carter campaign in Iowa, may have legitimized the precinct caucuses as a source of hard news for the news media.

Two presidential candidates, George McGovern and Jimmy Carter, used the caucuses effectively in order to gain media attention for their campaigns, and in the process they contributed to Iowa's growth as a media event. McGovern, realizing that the early date for the 1972 precinct caucuses could attract media attention, quietly organized a grass-roots Iowa campaign that brought coverage from national news organizations. After an exploratory trip to the state in 1975, Carter decided to launch an all-out effort in the precinct caucuses. When it began to appear that his organizational effort might pay dividends, it was in Carter's interest to turn the caucuses into a media event to maximize the surprise of an Iowa victory, should one occur. Apple was very helpful in that regard.

Working behind the scenes to make the Democratic caucuses a media event was the state Democratic party, and particularly the state chair, Tom Whitney. He and party staffers cooperated with the presidential hopefuls to gain press exposure for the candidates' 1976 campaigns in Iowa. The party made every effort to accommodate the media demand for evidence of the progress of the presidential campaign, including holding preference polls and providing timely statewide results of the caucus process. Whitney's efforts proved mutually beneficial to the party, the media, and the candidates, because each gained something from the increased visibility of the precinct caucuses.

The multiple efforts of party, press, and presidential

candidates were so successful in turning the Iowa caucuses into a media event that by 1980 Iowa rivaled New Hampshire for prominence as a nominating event. But along the way the promoters conveniently lost sight of the fact that caucus and convention systems do not produce outcomes in the way that primary elections do. There are no votes for presidential candidates; the only voting that takes place is for delegates to succeeding levels in the process. The Iowa Republican and Democratic parties dealt with the "results problem" in different ways, but essentially both contrived or manufactured results for the media. However, because Iowa selects delegates in its caucus and convention process, the media attribute more meaning to its results than to those in states that hold isolated presidential polls or "beauty contests." Contrived Iowa results are reported as if they were comparable to the outcomes of the New Hampshire primary rather than the Vermont straw poll.

The research presented here shows that the Iowa results are neither valid nor reliable indicators of the presidential preferences of delegates selected to succeeding levels in the caucus and convention process, and Republican leaders make little claim that they are. There is a long tradition—perhaps a slowly evolving one—that Republican caucuses do not require those who seek to represent their precincts at county conventions to disclose their candidate preferences. Some Republicans claim, however, that their caucus poll is more than a beauty contest because it includes the pool of Republicans from which county delegates are selected. Presumably this ties the poll, however nebulously, to delegate selection. This contention seems to stretch a point, since without a knowledge of candidate preferences it is impossible to determine if those delegates elected to county conventions are representative of the sentiments of the larger caucus poll.

Iowa Democrats go to great lengths to make their results meaningful. With scientific precision they use proportional representation, a 15 percent viability rule, and a weighting factor for each county to overcome variations in county convention sizes. Rather than releasing to the news media the weighted county delegates for each candidate— which admittedly is not a readily understandable concept—Democratic leaders add to the confusion by calling these figures "state delegate equivalents." They also project each candidate's strength at the state convention— called "projected state delegates"—and at the Democratic National Convention several months in the future—termed "national delegate equivalents." Presumably, projections of state and national delegates are more newsworthy than weighted county delegates, but they, too, are very misleading, since an assumption of the projections is that campaign conditions will remain constant between the February caucuses and the state and national conventions the following summer. This has proved to be a very poor assumption, for two reasons: first, neither party "binds" its delegates at succeeding levels in the process; and second, as the political process is played out at the county, district, and state levels and as the field of presidential candidates narrows, there is fluctuation in candidate support, particularly when the number of presidential hopefuls is large. Projecting levels of national delegate strength after the first stage in a fluid multistage process is untenable. The Democrats' delegate projections are little more than guesses. Similarly, the Republican precinct straw poll is not tied to delegate selection and is little more than a "beauty contest."

Perhaps more serious than misleading projections is the lack of independent controls over the tabulation and release of caucus outcomes. In Iowa, unlike states holding primary elections in which third parties administer the electoral process, the political parties conduct, collect, and process their own caucus results. With no independent check, Iowa parties have doctored the results to help build a media event (the Democrats in 1976, for example) and have reported highly questionable outcomes to the news media (the Republicans in 1980). The plain and simple fact is that Iowa parties can report what they please. By 1984 the news media were skeptical enough of the results the Iowa parties provided to hire an independent vote-counting service (the News Election Service) to tabulate caucus outcomes, but due to the dynamic and nonelectoral nature of the Democratic process the NES effort was not very successful.

The Iowa precinct caucuses have been turned into a mediality in every sense of Robinson's use of the term. The basically local functions of the caucuses are obscured by the practice of featuring the meetings as an early test in the horse race for the nomination. Fueled by the interdependent relationship that has developed between Iowa's parties, the press, and the presidential candidates, the contrived nature of the event and the lack of meaningful results are glossed over. Media exploitation of the caucus process subjects the nation and the political process to the influence of a contrived event, and the reporting of meaningless results—definitely phony results in 1976 and perhaps erroneous results in 1980—may give a false image of the national political appeal of the candidates involved. George Bush was able to secure the vice-presidential nomination in part as a result of the tremendous boost he received from the perception that he had upset Ronald Reagan in Iowa in 1980—a victory based on figures that are of questionable accuracy according to those who did the vote tabulation.

But the popularity and influence of the precinct caucuses continues, largely because their transformation into a national event has benefited those who helped to create it. Iowa has benefited from the national publicity surrounding the caucuses and the numerous in-depth stories about the state and its people, the caucuses have generated large sums of money for the state's businesses, and the national attention has helped the Iowa Democratic and Republican parties by stimulating interest and participation in the caucus process. State officials of both parties are pleased to identify sources of citizen support nine or ten months before the November election. They are also pleased by the increased status accorded the parties and their leaders, some of whom have been quoted in national publications such as *Time* and *Newsweek*. The media have benefited from the fact that the caucuses provide them with early "evidence" of the progress of the various presidential campaigns. The early indicator helps the media to define and label the status of presidential contenders. Finally, the caucuses afford presidential candidates who are relatively unknown a testing ground for their candidacies. In Iowa, they can run an old-fashioned grass-roots campaign on a relatively modest budget and, if successful, gain extensive favorable national exposure.

There are also potential disadvantages to Iowa's new national status. In 1980 large numbers of political "amateurs," stimulated by precaucus publicity, attended and participated in the meetings. Some people who were attending their first caucus were elected delegates to county conventions. Should too many party regulars be crowded out by amateurs whose interest may wax and wane, local party organization could eventually suffer. Iowa Democrats also sued each other over the date of the 1984 meetings, which is hardly a party-building exercise.

A potentially greater disadvantage lies in the possibility of Iowa becoming a pawn in the national electoral process. The "nationalization" of politics leads to outside money, outside issues, and simply outsiders injecting themselves into local politics. The effect is to distract local politics from local issues while causing the national candidates to play out their roles on a very limited and bucolic stage.

From a national perspective, perhaps the stage is too small. Iowa sent 58 Democratic and 37 Republican delegates to the national conventions in 1984, and they represented only 1.5 and 1.7 percent of the respective delegate totals. Before the caucuses became media events, participants in them typically represented less than 10 percent of the registered voters, although this figure grew to about 20

Iowa has become a pawn in the national electoral process. It provides a stage where the winnowing process for the presidential campaign can be played. David Yepsen, political columnist for the *Des Moines Register*, has suggested that a great deal of campaign time and money could be saved by building the facade of a typical Iowa farm at the Des Moines airport. Candidates could then give their agriculture speech and appear in a farm environment for rolling TV cameras without leaving the airport.

percent in 1980 before tapering off in 1984. Iowa has only eight electoral votes.

Iowa is a small, homogeneous, midwestern farm state largely composed of small cities and rural areas. The political culture and demography of Iowa may be typical of the midwestern agricultural heartland, but an aging population and the lack of major urban centers, substantial minority populations, and diversity in general make it a poor mirror of the national political culture, particularly that of the Democratic party.

Although no state can legitimately claim to mirror the national electorate, Iowa is less representative than many. Larger states justifiably complain that Iowa influences the candidate selection process far more than it should, given its lack of demographic and political representativeness. There is a certain irony in the fact that a state that supported the Republican candidate for president in eight of the last nine general elections has come to play a decisive role in the selection of the Democratic nominee.

Representative or not, the Iowa caucuses have become an important part of the presidential nominating game. It matters little that Iowa is not a microcosm of the United States or that the "results" of the precinct caucuses suffer problems of validity and reliability. The name of the presidential nominating game is perception, and the reality of the Iowa precinct caucuses has long been replaced by the media perception of them. It is not the caucus event per se but the media report of the event that shapes the presidential selection process—just as earlier it was not so much the event itself but the report of the event that shaped the politics of Watergate and Vietnam. Iowa is first. The precinct caucuses provide early evidence—hard news—on the progress of the presidential race. This is the perception of Iowa's role, and it is therefore the reality of the precinct caucuses.

Extensive media coverage changes the nature of the political process, and nowhere more conspicuously than in the presidential selection process. As described by Patterson, the modern presidential race is a media campaign. The media have become the principal linkage between candidates and voters in national campaigns, and voters have grown to rely on the media for an interpretation of, as well as information about, the political campaigns. In the process, the media have become not only reporters of the news but also important actors in the electoral process. They identify the candidates for the American public; by emphasis or neglect they decide which issues are important; they are instrumental in establishing a set of expectations about the candidates' likelihood of success; they evaluate the progress of the race according to the expectations they help to create; and finally, they determine the "winners" and "losers," again according to their own expectations.

The drama or excitement in presidential elections is provided by the horse race, and to have a race requires at least two candidates. For good drama, a close two- or three-person race is ideal. Too many candidates make analysis and handicapping difficult, thus the need for events like Iowa to winnow the field; but a race with only one horse draws few readers and viewers. Thus the presidential game is an unreliable game; the race might end too early. The 1984 Democratic contest is a good example. Mondale *was* the Iowa caucus story—his totals exceeded the delegate equivalents of the other seven candidates combined—but the handicappers found a few surprises in the stronger-than-expected finishes of McGovern and Hart, and choosing to go with Hart, made him the other horse in the race even though his share of the delegate totals was only 16.5 percent. Later Jesse Jackson, who represented another dimension in the drama, was taken seriously by the media.

The evaluation of caucus and primary outcomes is a complex process based on the perceptions of reporters who seldom report in a straightforward way that, for example, candidate A received 49 percent of the vote and candidate B 17 percent. A candidate who receives the most delegates or votes is not always declared the winner, and candidates who do not do well in an absolute sense are not always called losers. Rather, those labels are assigned according to how well candidates fulfill their assigned roles. Mondale's 1984 victory was significant because he met the very high expectations of his front-runner role; Carter in 1976 and Bush in 1980 were "surprise winners" because they were perceived to have fared much better than expected. The perception of losing is equally important. Candidates who fail to meet the expectations of their roles are quickly dismissed by the media. The handicappers were certain that Ted Kennedy posed a real threat to Jimmy Carter in 1980 and thought John Glenn would be a serious challenger in 1984. When Kennedy's and Glenn's shares of the delegate equivalents were much less than expected in Iowa, they were virtually dismissed as viable candidates.

It is on the basis of such limited evidence that the media judge some candidates winners and others losers and begin the winnowing process. Thus, contrived media events like the Iowa caucuses, with their straw polls and delegate equivalents, take on a life of their own and become significant events in the electoral process. Due to their status as media events, they command the attention of presidential candidates, and 1984 demonstrated that candidates will not repeat Reagan's 1980 mistake of underestimating the impact of the Iowa caucuses.

Since 1972 Iowa has played an ever-larger role in the presidential nominating game by providing the first hard news for the media. By adapting their caucuses to media needs, Iowa's parties have become willing and influential players in the media-choreographed contest for the presidency. Media attention has grown geometrically, and Iowa now rivals New Hampshire for the title of presidential kingmaker.

The impact of the caucuses on the presidential nominating process is further demonstrated by the success of caucus "winners" since Iowa became a media event. Carter and Ford, the 1976 winners, went on to cap-

Duffy 2-20-84

The precinct caucuses have made Iowa a major player in the presidential nominating contest. Iowa now rivals New Hampshire for the attention of presidential candidates, and shortly after President Reagan's reelection in 1984, Congressman Richard Gephardt of Missouri was already appearing in Iowa in preparation for his 1988 bid for the Democratic presidential nomination.

ture their parties' nomination, and in 1980 Carter's "big victory" over Kennedy in the Democratic caucuses led to his renomination. Even George Bush, the 1980 Republican straw poll leader fared well, becoming his party's vice-presidential nominee. The 1984 caucuses gave Mondale a big win, but the media interpretation of the Iowa results also kept the Hart campaign alive.

Iowa is also a major reason for the front-loading of the presidential campaign. Other state parties, envious of the status afforded Iowa and New Hampshire, have moved their nominating events closer to the beginning of the thirteen-week primary schedule. The result is a skewed, or front-loaded, primary schedule dominated by small and unrepresentative states like Iowa. The impact of these early events is great: In 1984, five of the eight Democratic candidates had withdrawn from the race within a month after the Iowa caucuses.

Iowa also has contributed to the trivialization of the nominating process. The results of the Iowa process are unreliable, but that is overlooked by the media in their fervid quest for hard news. Media interpretations, often based on contrived events like Iowa, become the reality of presidential campaigns and determine the rules by which the candidates play the game.

The American public deserves better. In the Iowa media event, the state parties, the presidential candidates, and the national and local media pursue their individual agendas. Each has a stake in maintaining the caucuses as a national event. There is no creative tension between the actors. Rather, there is cooperation and collusion to perpetuate what is in effect a fraud. The public interest is not well served when manipulated and distorted nominating events like the Iowa precinct caucuses determine the viability of presidential candidacies.

Index